Problem Tenants in Public Housing

Richard S. Scobie

The Praeger Special Studies program—utilizing the most modern and efficient book production techniques and a selective worldwide distribution network—makes available to the academic, government, and business communities significant, timely research in U.S. and international economic, social, and political development.

Problem Tenants in Public Housing

Who, Where, and
Why Are They?

PRAEGER SPECIAL STUDIES IN U.S. ECONOMIC, SOCIAL, AND POLITICAL ISSUES

Praeger Publishers   New York   Washington   London

Library of Congress Cataloging in Publication Data

Scobie, Richard S
    Problem tenants in public housing.

    (Praeger special studies in U.S. economic, social,
and political issues)
    Bibliography: p.
    Includes index.
    1. Public housing—United States. 2. Problem
family—United States. I. Title.
HD7293.S38   301.36   74-9425
ISBN 0-275-09580-0

PRAEGER PUBLISHERS
111 Fourth Avenue, New York, N.Y. 10003, U.S.A.
5, Cromwell Place, London SW7 2JL, England

Published in the United States of America in 1975
by Praeger Publishers, Inc.

Printed in the United States of America

to Jill

The problem of the "problem tenant" has been a personal concern of mine for over ten years. From my earliest experiences as a social worker and social planner in public housing neighborhoods, through the years in tenant organizing, and as director of a tenant relations and social service unit in a large metropolitan housing authority, I have been intrigued by the problem tenant and that elaborate web of myth, fact and emotion that surrounds it. We had all heard about "those families"—the ones presumably responsible for the multitude of ills that plague many low-income communities—and certainly one occasionally encountered a family whose collective behavior bordered on the notorious. Yet, as the catalogue of woes laid at the feet of those families grew in size, I began to feel uncomfortable with the whole concept.

Not only was there little agreement as to who those families really were or even a precise definition of how one qualified for the title; it was further clear that most of the tenant selection schemes that purported to "screen out" potential problem tenants did no such thing. My growing skepticism was strengthened during the ideological struggles of the middle 1960s when a combination of the tenant rights movement and a series of legal discussions began to challenge the moral legitimacy as well as the legality of many housing authority policies that denied access to housing or permitted eviction of families labeled "unsuitable."

The late 1960s saw a resurgence of more conservative social analysis and a renewed interest in problem definitions that emphasized the characterological deficiencies of individuals or social classes. With new theoretical (if not empirical) support from such academic notables as Edward Banfield of Harvard, it was not long before articles began to appear calling for more stringent tenant selection policies to screen out potential problem tenants (assuming they can be identified) and for more homogeneous neighborhoods, which would not attempt to mix presumably incompatible groups (as in Roger Starr's discussion of conflict between the "working poor" and the "dependent poor").

Between 1969 and 1972 I had an excellent opportunity to examine the problem of the problem tenant in considerable depth while studying at the Florence Heller School of Advanced Studies in Social Welfare at Brandeis University. In this I received invaluable assistance and counsel from David Austin, currently at the University of Texas at Austin, Norman Kurtz of Brandeis, Seymour Bellin of Tufts University, and Lisa Peattie of the Massachusetts Institute of Technology, who first inspired me to undertake this research. The study was initially written as a dissertation—a fact that greatly influenced its form and style. For greater readability much of the methodological description and the more detailed findings have been relocated in the appendixes.

Basically the study examines the phenomenon of the problem tenants (operationally defined as those tenants who are seen as problematic by management) in order to see: (1) just how prevalent the problem tenant is, (2) the extent to which people who are identified as problem tenants are also "problem families" (a diagnostic category involving whole constellations of problems), (3) the ways in which problem tenants differ from their neighbors (if they do), (4) the extent to which conflict among tenants is a factor in their being identified as problems by management, and (5) whether conflict among tenants was in any way associated with those social differences that have received such emphasis in popular discussion.

The findings were startling in their clarity and strongly suggest a reevaluation of the assumptions on which many current tenant selection and housing development policies are based. My hope is that this edition, in making these findings available to a wider audience, will stimulate planners and housing administrators to renew their debate over the problem tenant, and over all of the associated questions of population homogeneity and design about which we still know so little.

CONTENTS

LIST OF TABLES AND FIGURE

Problem Tenants in Public Housing

PROBLEM TENANTS IN PUBLIC HOUSING: AN OVERVIEW

PUBLIC HOUSING IN THE UNITED STATES—EARLY GOALS AND ASSUMPTIONS

The public housing program in the United States was born in that crucible of social welfare policy formulation known as the Great Depression. The Housing Act of 1937, which established the Federal role in this heretofore almost exclusively private activity, set in motion the basic financial mechanisms that were subsequently elaborated in the housing acts and amendments of following years. Although many of the earliest supporters of the program emphasized the social objectives of better housing, the primary thrust of the legislation was to help the national economy, to stimulate the building materials and construction industries, and to provide jobs.[1] It was, in fact, only one of the many programs that constituted the New Deal effort to end the depression. As such public housing was viewed in most circles as a "property program" rather than a social program.[2]

Writings of housing professionals in this period reflected an overriding concern with the technical problems of land acquisition, construction, and physical maintenance to the almost total exclusion of any comment on the social problems encountered in management. Even the pioneers who had been associated with preceding programs such as those constructed by the Works Progress Administration (WPA) between 1935 and 1937 neglected to discuss the social implications of their work.[3] This is not to imply that there was no sense of enthusiasm about the "good works" nature of the by-product; there was, in fact, an almost crusading spirit associated with the slum-clearance aspects of many projects. Wiping out blight caught the fancy of many of the participants during those early years, but the assumptions they held about the power of "safe, decent, sanitary" accommodations (as the Housing Act stated it) to ameliorate most social problems unassisted were as unshakable as they were naive.

1

THE HAPPY YEARS

To some extent, during the early years of the program, expectations of a relatively strife-free management task were rewarded. Prior to 1949 local housing authorities had virtually a free hand in the selection of tenants, and it was their practice to choose their residents very carefully. They tended to select a highly homogeneous and stable working-class tenant body, drawn frequently from second and third generation European immigrants, a group of "temporary poor" who, suffering from the state of the national economy, were grateful for the chance to obtain sound housing at a lower rent than they could get in the open market. Families that were "different"— female headed, of a minority race, or with attitudes that offended tenant selection personnel—were frequently screened out, ensuring a population that was largely "like-minded" with respect to one another and to the management. The developments themselves were usually constructed in stable working-class neighborhoods, further fixing their image and life style.

During World War II the national attention turned to the war effort, with public housing becoming a major mechanism for providing housing for the workers in war industries and the families of persons in the armed forces. This provided local authorities with a new supply of "worthy" tenants, working or middle class in life style, intact, and essentially homogeneous. With large numbers of eligible applicants, relatively few vacancies, and no legislation requiring them to accept "unworthy" or different persons, authorities were able to continue providing housing while avoiding involvement in social problems that might have emerged had they had a more heterogeneous tenant population.[4]

There were some early hints of problems to come. In the 1938 classic Diary of a Housing Manager, by Abraham Goldfeld,[5] there were frequent references to growing problems with vandalism, tenant conflicts, crime, and the need to seek out social agencies for assistance in isolated cases. While Goldfeld was an extremely sympathetic and sensitive manager, although rather paternalistic in the style of the day, he expresses frequent fears that he will begin to lose control of his tenant population:

> On my trips through the East Side I notice much vandalism and writing on the walls by the children. My estimate is that we will have between 200 and 300 children in the house. What to do to keep them out of mischief and from damaging the property? It is a great challenge.[6]

> The children already present a problem. They play
> very noisily in the courts until late at night. . . . Meas-
> ures must be taken immediately to check this type of
> disorder or it will become unmanageable.[7]

Goldfeld enjoyed a highly homogeneous and upwardly mobile tenant population. Nevertheless, the social difficulties that did arise led him to advise, writing with Beatrice Rosahn, that tenants should be carefully screened before selection.[8] For the next decade this was to be possible, but under the Housing Act of 1949 a new set of factors came into play.

THE END OF THE HAPPY YEARS

The Housing Act of 1949 ended the happy days of homogeneous tenant bodies and harmonious housing management by the following means: in Title I providing for massive slum clearance programs that were to displace diverse populations of very poor families; in Title II extending and broadening the federal mortgage insurance program, making it possible for working-class families who might otherwise have become public housing tenants to purchase their own homes; and in Title III both expanding the public housing program and introducing provisions that would limit the program to very low in-come families, assuring that displaced persons would get preference. Whereas in the 1930s local authorities were able to select only the most obvious "deserving" tenants, since 1949 they have had to take "whoever was displaced by some other government agency's action— usually those who would not and could not be housed by anyone else."[9] Most authorities tried to defend themselves by instituting more subtle screening procedures in order to retain their prerogatives, but gradually the impact of the 1949 act was felt.

This new mix of tenants changed the lives of housing managers almost everywhere, especially in cities that embarked on large urban renewal programs or other projects that required the relocation of large numbers of families. While there were many severely dis-organized families housed for the first time during this period, their numbers scarcely accounted for the sense of alarm that spread through the ranks of the professional housers. The new developments built under the 1949 act were housing their first occupants when a debate broke out nationally over what to do about families that were presumed to be disrupting the social fabric.

Encouraged by simultaneous developments in the social welfare field that focused attention on a phenomenon called the "problem family" (see Chapter 2 for a detailed discussion of this topic), housing

3

professionals argued among themselves over what could be done about them and over the extent to which they were legally or morally responsible for doing anything at all. In the housing field there were both "hardliners" who held that public housing should only accept "normal" families that could demonstrate the ability to meet certain standards of behavior before admission,[10] and "softliners" who believed that housing authorities were responsible for the provision of social services and rehabilitative programs for their tenants when they needed them.[11] What both hardliners and softliners agreed upon was that the problem family was the cause of many of management's problems.

The Committee on Management of the National Association of Housing and Redevelopment Officials (NAHRO) stated in August 1955 that: "in the main 'problem' families have replaced 'normal' families in public housing," and called for the recognition by management of its "prime responsibility" to organize its operations in such a way that the special problems of these families could be addressed.[12] The prescribed treatment varied depending on the theories that were dominant at any given time about the cause of problem families. In general, most housers agreed with NAHRO that they needed the "full assistance of the public and private community agencies staffed by people skilled in casework or rehabilitation work,"[13] although they disagreed among themselves about the specific role that was appropriate for housing officials.

RESPONSES TO TENANT PROBLEMS AND PROBLEM TENANTS

The responses of housing management personnel and of community health and welfare agencies to this challenge were diverse, but all aimed at the identification and rehabilitation of problem families through various combinations of casework, education, training in home economics and child care, and isolation. In the late 1950s and early 1960s "experimental" programs sprang up in several cities.[1] The housing authority in Syracuse created a new position on its staff, that of "coordinator of social services," whose job it was to consult with housing personnel and to organize social and recreational service in the housing developments. In Washington, D.C., the local welfare department was induced to locate its field offices in housing projects in order to make their caseworkers more easily accessible. Cincinnati emphasized community organization approaches to bring the services of a range of social agencies to bear on the needs of the projects. In Gary, Indiana, with the help of the education department, home economics training was offered and in Columbus, Missouri, "extension agents" from the Department of Agriculture were used to orient new tenants to the use of the buildings, appliances, and so forth. In Boston several disciplines were brought together in a multiservice center in one development, staffed by a community organizer, a home economist, a family caseworker, and an "area youth worker" with group work training.[15]

Simultaneously, NAHRO formed a Committee on Social Work in Housing and Urban Renewal. In 1962 it published a widely read monograph that described programs dealing with problem families in many cities, stressing the necessity of including social services in both urban renewal and housing agencies.[16] This philosophy was taken up and supported by the then Federal Commissioner of Public Housing Marie McGuire, who encouraged local authorities to add social service personnel to their rosters. Although these moves tended to be resisted by hardliners throughout the federal bureaucracy as well as at the local level, many of the larger authorities added "social service coordinators," "management aides," "tenant relations aides," and "tenant relations departments" to their staffs.

Funds were never plentiful enough to enable housing authorities to hire more than a handful of such personnel; so the prevailing policy emphasized "community responsibility" for providing social services in housing development neighborhoods. Since the response of most communities fell far short of the perceived need, the Department of Health, Education, and Welfare (HEW) and the Housing and Home Finance Agency (HHFA—the predecessor of the Department of Housing and Urban Development) created a Joint Task Force on Health, Education, and Welfare Services and Housing in 1963. This task force aimed to show what was possible when agencies on the local level worked together in alliance with the federal bureaucracies, employing a mixture of local and national funding.

With several millions of dollars available, four "concerted services" projects were launched; in St. Louis, New Haven, Pittsburgh (California), and Miami. The members of the federal task force pointed out that there was a range of federally funded programs dealing with almost every imaginable social problem. If these were focused in a coordinated way upon the needs of specific communities, it was argued that the assembled resources would surely constitute an effective force for reducing social problems. Although some of the publications developed as a part of this effort were useful[17] and the experience a valuable preview of some of the difficulties that were to accompany the "war on poverty" which followed, the results of the demonstrations were disappointing.[18] The programs in both HEW and HHFA proved stubbornly resistant to coordination, and the difficulties encountered in trying to synchronize the approval of grants by diverse bureaus and departments left the participants happy to surrender the field to the Office of Economic Opportunity (OEO) and local community action agencies in 1964.

Meanwhile, a team of social scientists and social workers at the Syracuse University Youth Development Center were at work trying to identify the precise differences between "stable" and "problem" families living in certain local housing projects.* Charles Willie and Janet Weinandy, in discussing some of their findings, argued that problem families were "uncommitted to the value system of a monogamous society," living "unregulated lives," "inadequately socialized" for "participation in human social organization."[19] Although commentators on this research, including Lee Rainwater, challenged the conclusions as unsubstantiated by the data,[20] the general view of problem tenants as uniquely pathological was reinforced.

During this period the studies at Syracuse were widely read in housing circles, and their prescription of aggressive casework with problem families utilizing the external controls available through public authorities was to become a part of many rehabilitative programs launched in public housing in the mid-1960s.†

The European Response

Housing management's pursuit of the problem family was not limited to this side of the Atlantic. In Europe, especially since the end of World War II, there has been activity on the part of housing

---

*Charles Willie and Janet Weinandy, "The Structure and Composition of 'Problem' and 'Stable' Families in Low-Income Populations," Marriage and Family Living, November 1963. pp. 439-47.

Including in the category of problem family only those with dependent children under 21 years of age, they selected their study group by asking the manager to list those families that he considered to be "problem families" and "in need of help." He identified 56 out of 678 households (or 8 percent), along with 40 families he considered to be stable. The groups were then compared, showing the problem group, which included a higher proportion of female-headed families, with younger heads, more children, and a history of earlier marriage. All of these characteristics were seen as effects rather than causes of instability by the researchers, who reported evidence of "uncontrolled, impulsive behavior" in the problem-family group.

†The Public Housing Administration, NAHRO, and the National Federation of Settlements conducted many regional workshops during this period, in which the Syracuse studies received a great deal of attention.

administrators, social workers, and governmental bodies all aimed
at the speedy identification of families that were potential problems
and their effective rehabilitation. In their search for strategies and
alternative treatment programs, European officials had two advantages
over their American colleagues: (1) the extreme housing shortages
produced by the devastation of the war made the public housing program frequently the only possible source of housing for low-income
families; (2) paternalism was accepted as an appropriate style of
operation for public officials. Thus one finds extremely authoritarian
programs in Europe that would simply not be feasible in the United
States.[21]

In England prior screening was used extensively in attempts to
identify the problem family. Officials appeared to search mainly
for poor housekeepers and classified from one to two percent of their
families in this way;[22] these families were placed first in older, less
desirable public housing. While in this temporary halfway house they
would be subjected to intensive social-service and educational programs designed to bring their functioning up to an acceptable level.
The incentive was, of course, a chance at being rehoused in more
adequate, newer accommodations also owned by the public authority.

In Scotland several towns experimented with complete isolation
of families identified as problems in therapeutic settings for rehabilitation. Perth, Midlothian, and Paisley have all been using this technique
for years with marginal success[23] but have been severely criticized
by housing councils elsewhere in the United Kingdom who have pointed
out the stigmatizing effect of prolonged segregation of families.[24]
One area of agreement in Great Britain seems to be the unsatisfactory
nature of eviction as a solution. There seems to be consensus that
the community has a responsibility to all families, especially those
with children, and that therefore some kind of housing must be provided regardless of the family characteristics.[25]

In the Netherlands during the postwar period was begun the
development of many "reeducation" centers for "socially weak" families presumably unable to live responsibly in regular housing. Here
also one observes a level of paternalism and a use of authority that
would be unacceptable in the United States made possible not only
by the extreme shortage of housing but also by the homogeneous nature
of the Dutch nation.[26] When there is almost universal agreement
regarding norms of behavior, life style, and so on, it is possible to
quickly identify and isolate the "deviant" and subject him to special
"treatment." Although the programs in the Netherlands which have
specialized in segregated housing units for problem families have
been viewed with great interest by hard-pressed American housing
administrators, these techniques have not been successfully imported.

American Methods of Identifying Problem
Families

American officials have not been helpless, however. Though unable to sweep their problem families (or the ones they have identified as such) into a relatively neat, segregated facility, they have used other tools. Among these have been preadmission screening, selective enforcement of rules, and the use of eviction.

Irwin Deutscher's description of the director of tenant selection in public housing as the "gatekeeper" is a classic description of the way in which public officials, often with little or no personal commitment to the objectives of the program, have been able to screen out applicants using ritualistic or class-oriented judgments.[27] The director of tenant selection under observation in that study made subjective judgments regarding the desirability of applicants, as well as the degree of their need for housing and the priority they should consequently hold. In judging desirability, she relied heavily on the manner of speech and dress of the applicant, reflecting her own middle-class background and values. She also considered race, family composition, and the attitude of the applicant during the interview. Even among those she felt were acceptable, she made finer judgments regarding their desirability, sending the "best" families to the "best" projects. These practices have been widespread in public housing, and only recently have they begun to be challenged by civil rights groups, antipoverty lawyers, and tenants' rights organizations as discussed below.

Once a tenant is in occupancy, a housing authority has less room to maneuver but nonetheless retains some options. The threat of eviction is always available, as are social service referrals insofar as competent agencies exist in the community. These are both used on occasion, the mix depending on the temperament and training of the manager, the pressure he may or may not be under to take action, the "attractiveness" and attitudes of the family in question, and the degree of tolerance in the community at large. As Bitner has described in his discussion of police practices,[28] public officials enforce rules and regulations selectively. Housing officials are no exception. This has been especially true in the decisions regarding which tenants to evict, as the study by Lempert and Ikeda has shown.[29] Frequently responding to bureaucratic pressures or complaints of other tenants, managers in the past have evicted tenants who were troublesome, either as nuisances, when this was possible, or simply for being in arrears in their rent.

Until quite recently local authorities have remained relatively unchallenged in their frequently arbitrary use of these devices. As recently as 1963 the courts affirmed the power of a housing authority

8

to terminate tenancy with only a 15-day written notice, without citing reasons.[30] On the question of new applicants, the federal agency traditionally adopted a hands-off attitude and, except for auditing financial eligibility, left tenant selection standards up to local authorities. In one of the first challenges to the use of "desirability standards" to deny admission, in 1966 the courts upheld the right of the New York City Housing Authority to refuse to house a family because of the husband's record of juvenile arrests and convictions.[31] The court did, however, caution that their judgment applies in cases where there was an "established pattern" of questionable behavior, and that evidence of a "single incident" could no longer be sufficient cause for refusal.

Beginning of Challenges

The picture began to change drastically in 1967 when, encouraged and supported by OEO legal assistance lawyers, the number and intensity of challenges to arbitrary housing authority practices regarding admissions and evictions increased. The first serious reversal for local officials came in Thomas et al. vs. The Housing Authority of the City of Little Rock, Arkansas, in which the court held that the housing authority could not deny access or evict a family solely because a member has one or more illegitimate children.[32] This was followed a year later by Holmes vs. New York City Housing Authority, which held that the authority "must employ a reasonable and consistent system of selecting nonpreference candidates for low-income housing."*

On the question of evictions there was a period of great confusion in the late 1960s in which contradictory opinions were rendered in several different states.† But gradually a pattern was established

---

*Holmes vs. New York City Housing Authority, 398 F.2d 262, July 18, 1968. Cited in Journal of Housing, February 1969, p. 84. The court, noting that some families had sought housing in state and local projects over a period of six years, held that "due process" at least required "some consistent method of selection" other than the uncontrolled discretion of a public authority.

†See Chicago Housing Authority vs. Stewart, 237 N.E. 2d, 463, May 29, 1958, which held that no reasons were necessary for eviction; Vinson vs. Greenburgh Housing Authority, 288 N.Y.S. 2d 159, March 11, 1968, which held that reasons were necessary; Lancaster Housing Authority vs. Gardner, 211 Pennsylvania Superior Court 502, 240 A.2d 566, March 8, 1968, which held reasons couldn't be challenged.

that affirmed the rights of tenants as opposd to the prerogatives of local housing authorities. Landmark decisions were Thorpe vs. Housing Authority of Durham, North Carolina, which, upheld by the U.S. Supreme Court, reversed earlier opinions that local housing authorities could evict tenants arbitrarily without notice,[33] and Caulder vs. Housing Authority of Durham, North Carolina, which, expanding on the Thorpe decision, required a hearing before an impartial board in which the accused tenant would have an opportunity to confront those testifying against him.[34]

In response to these opinions and to pressures from the newly formed National Tenants Organization, the Department of Housing and Urban Development (HUD) published circulars on grievance and eviction procedures that for the first time began to spell out specific steps expected of local authorities in handling these cases.[35] While a recent opinion in New York denying a hearing to rejected applicants for housing may signal the end of the "pro-tenant" period of the preceding three years,[36] the principles established in the Thomas, Holmes, Thorpe, and Caulder cases have clearly limited the power of housing authorities to determine the social characteristics of their tenant bodies. On the power to evict, the last serious challenge to the liberal trend was that of the Housing Authority of Omaha in its attempt to overthrow the HUD grievance procedures on the grounds that they were in violation of the principle of local autonomy. Although the Authority won at the district level, that decision was overruled in Federal Circuit Court,[37] and, though frequently unenforced, the grievance procedures still stand.

THE NEW PESSIMISM

The late 1960s saw a growing dissatisfaction with the traditional approach to problem tenants, which had defined them as a pathological category of families that should be screened out, treated and rehabilitated, or eliminated through eviction. Regardless of errors along these lines, the proportion of alleged problem families, the difficulties of managers with problem tenants, and the whole range of tenant-related management problems seemed not to be diminishing but rather increasing.

Initial disillusionment was primarily the result of a lack of effectiveness of social services in eliminating the problem of the problem tenant. As George Shermer noted in his 1967 report to NAHRO, not only are social services highly fragmented and under-manned but the services themselves are simply not as valuable as they have been assumed to be.[38] Citing Janet Weinandy's observation that traditional therapeutic approaches to low-income clients are

10

often simply not applicable, he went beyond her cautionary comments to throw doubt upon the entire social service approach to these problems. In doing so, however, he continued to focus upon the families themselves, presuming the presence of a high degree of pathology in the tenant population to be the true cause of management's difficulties.

In his later report for the National Commission on Urban Problems, Shermer concentrated on the changing social composition of public housing and expressed his concern that, with a substantial shift in national policy to rent supplements and related schemes, public housing will increasingly house the very poor, the displaced, and those with serious emotional and behavioral problems.[39] Still devoted to the "problem family" explanation, he had to fall back again on a prescription for more federally financed social services attached to each housing development.[40]

The 1970s have seen a shift in the national mood, especially as it is reflected in the popular analysis of social problems. Heretofore liberal commentators and scholars have expressed what might be characterized as a "new pessimism" regarding social phenomena, including the problem tenant. In his Unheavenly City, Edward Banfield dwelled once again on the alleged moral inadequacy of the "lower class," which he defined as those people who are unable to defer gratification or to provide for the future.[41] He attributed most urban problems to this group, and his prescriptions usually emphasized segregation or isolation. A more recent and perhaps more serious elaboration of this analysis was Roger Starr's article, "Which of the Poor Shall Live in Public Housing," which appeared in The Public Interest early in 1971.[42]

Starr, a long-time champion of public programs in housing and development, bemoans the physical and social deterioration of the public housing program in New York City and elsewhere and attributes it to the exit of the "working poor" before a virtual invasion by the "non-working, dependent poor." It is this latter group that he asserts (admittedly without supporting data) contributes most heavily to vandalism and is responsible for the greatest amount of crime both on the streets and inside the projects.[43] This dependent group, like Banfield's lower class, is not merely economically different from other groups but also different in its whole attitude toward work and life and in its behavior. He thus expands the pathological explanation of problem tenants from the relatively narrow concern with problem families that dominated the thinking of the previous two decades to an entire class of problem families: the dependent poor. More precisely, he identifies the fatherless, female-headed household receiving Aid to Families with Dependent Children (AFDC) as the source of management's problems.

THE INTENT OF THE STUDY

It is the intent of this study to question the traditional assumption that problem tenants are necessarily problem families, or that factors leading to a tenant's becoming a problem to management are necessarily pathological. By examining the social characteristics of families that are actually considered by housing managers to be problems, as well as their nature and distribution and the process by which they are identified, this study will attempt to develop more satisfactory explanations for the existence of problem tenants.

Before proceeding, two disclaimers should be offered. First, this study will not argue that social services are an inappropriate or superfluous component of management's responsibility. On the contrary, social services are a necessity when one is housing any such highly vulnerable population. When a family lives close to the margin, economically and otherwise, crises can be devastating, and an array of social services can go a long way toward helping such a family to weather the frequent storms with minimal suffering. Occasionally certain families can be helped to function more satisfactorily and to overcome self-destructive perceptions and patterns of behavior. Nevertheless, this paper suggests that to expect these services to deal with the management problem of problem tenants may be unjustified, not because services are of limited effectiveness in dealing with problem families but rather because the problem family explanation of what creates a problem tenant is inadequate and may not accurately describe reality. Second, the study has been executed from the perspective of management: it is concerned with their task as they perceive it and with those tenants that managers see as being problems to them. It is recognized that an alternative might have been to study the interaction of managers and tenants, adopting the perspective of tenants and stressing their perceptions of management and of its role, responsibilities, and performance vis-à-vis tenants. This, however interesting, would be quite another study and not the one undertaken here.

As William Gamson has suggested, there are two essentially distinct points of view in most social situations, particularly where formal organizations such as a public housing authority are involved: the perspective of the "authorities," those able to make binding decisions; and that of the "potential partisans," those seeking to influence those same decisons.[44] Housing managers are, of necessity, cast in the role of authorities and, as such, are concerned about the issue of social control. This is their lot, whether they are appointed by a public authority or elected from among the tenant body as may be the case if current tenant management experiments are successful. Regardless of the person occupying the manager's office, the responsibilities placed upon him or her will require certain decisions and uses of authority in respect to the tenant population. This study hopes to clarify the nature of that group of decisions surrounding the problem tenant and to suggest some alternatives to those strategies that have already been employed with such limited success.

NOTES

1. See the discussions of this period in Charles Abrams, The City is the Frontier (New York: Harper and Row, 1965); Glen H. Beyer, Housing: A Factual Analysis (New York: Macmillan, 1958): Glen H. Beyer, Housing and Society (New York: Macmillan, 1965): Leonard Freedman, Public Housing, the Politics of Poverty (New York: Holt, Rinehart and Winston, 1969): Martin Meyerson, Barbara Terrett, and William L. C. Wheaton, Housing, People and Cities (New York: McGraw Hill, 1962): Alvin L. Schorr, Slums and Social Insecurity (Washington, D.C.: Department of Health, Education and Welfare, 1963); George Shermer, More than Shelter: Social Needs in Low and Moderate Income Housing (Washington D.C.: Report to the Commission on Urban Problems, Research Report No. 8, 1968).

2. Shermer, op. cit., p. 6.

3. See National Association of Housing Officials, Housing Yearbooks, 1936, 1937, 1938.

4. Glen H. Beyer, Housing and Society (New York: Macmillan Co., 1965), pp. 252 ff.

5. Abraham Goldfeld, Diary of a Housing Manager (Chicago: NAHRO, 1938).

6. Ibid., p. 13.

7. Ibid., p. 19.

8. Beatrice Rosahn and Abraham Goldfeld, Housing Management Principles and Practices (Chicago: Covici Friede, 1937), p. 33.

9. Meyerson, op. cit., p. 300.

10. Bernard R. Seiler, "Problem Families Must Meet Standards Before Admission," Journal of Housing, February 1956, p. 66.

11. David Filker, "Public Housing Management Must Accept Family Rehabilitation Responsibility," Journal of Housing, May 1956, p. 168.

12. NAHRO Management Committee Report, cited in Journal of Housing, August and September 1955.

13. Ibid., as cited by Janet Weinandy and Lee Cary, Working with the Poor (Syracuse: Syracuse University Press, 1965), p. 3.

14. Journal of Housing, November 1959, pp. 363-66.

15. Albert Boer, The Community Service Center, mimeographed (Boston: United South End Settlements, 1961).

16. National Association of Housing and Redevelopment Officials, Change for the Better (Washington, D.C.: 1962).

17. Department of Health, Education, and Welfare and Housing and Home Finance Agency Joint Task Force on Health, Education, and Welfare Services and Housing, Services for Families Living in Public Housing (Washington, D.C.: 1963).

18. Department of Health, Education, and Welfare and Housing and Home Finance Agency Joint Task Force on Health, Education, and Welfare Services and Housing, Two Year Progress Report (Washington, D.C.: 1964).

19. Charles Willie and Janet Weinandy, "The Structure and Composition of 'Problem' and 'Stable' Families in Low-Income Populations," Marriage and Family Living, November 1963, pp. 444-46.

20. Lee Rainwater, comments on Willie and Weinandy, op. cit., p. 446.

21. Abner D. Silverman, Administration of Publicly Owned Housing (Great Britain, Netherlands, and Sweden) (Washington, D.C.: Housing and Home Finance Agency, U.S. Government Printing Office, 1961).

22. Abner D. Silverman, "Problem Families—Efforts at Social Rehabilitation Yield Results in Britain," Journal of Housing, February 1961, pp. 63-70.

23. Abner D. Silverman, Administration, op. cit., pp. 165-72.

24. Ministry of Housing and Local Government, Unsatisfactory Tenants (London: Her Majesty's Stationary Office, 1955), p. 14.

25. Silverman, "Problem Families," op. cit., pp. 68-69, and Administration, op. cit., p. 14.

26. Municipal Welfare Department of Rotterdam, the Netherlands, Zuidplein Project, 1953 and 1957; Ministry of Cultural Affairs, Recreation and Social Welfare, the Netherlands, Overijssel Family Re-Adaptation Center, 1967; Social Work Related to Problem Families and Neighborhoods in the Netherlands, 1966. All mimeographed.

27. Irwin Deutscher, "The Gatekeeper in Public Housing," in Irwin Deutscher and Elizabeth Thompson, Among the People: Encounters with the Poor (New York: Basic Books, 1968), pp. 38-52.

28. Egon Bitner, "The Police on Skid Row: A Study of Peace Keeping," American Sociological Review, October 1967, pp. 699-715.

29. Richard Lempert and Kiyoshi Ikeda, "Evictions from Public Housing: Effects of Independent Review," American Sociological Review, October 1970, pp. 852-59.

30. Cleveland Metropolitan Housing Authority vs. Patterson, Ohio Court of Appeals, Cuyahoga Country, July 10, 1963. This case, cited in Journal of Housing, August 1964, p. 384, confirmed an earlier opinion in Brand vs. Chicago Housing Authority, 120 F.2d 786-88, 1941.

31. Maringo vs. New York City Housing Authority, No. 2197/ 1966, Superior Court of New York, August 8, 1966. Affirmed, U.S. District Court, 279 New York State, 2d 1014, February 28, 1967.

32. Thomas et al. vs. Housing Authority of the City of Little Rock, U.S. District Court, Eastern District of Arkansas, May 26, 1967. 35 U. S. L. W. 272.

33. Thorpe vs. Housing Authority of Durham, 383 U.S. 268, January 13, 1969. Mrs. Thorpe had been evicted the day after her election as chairman of the tenants association. Cited in Journal of Housing, January 1969, p. 35.

34. Caulder vs. Durham Housing Authority, 433 F. 2d 998, 4th Cir. 1970. Cited in Journal of Housing, March 1971, p. 141.

35. U. S. Department of Housing and Urban Development, Renewal and Housing Management, Transmittal Notice: Grievance Procedures, RHM 7465-9, February 22, 1971. See also Journal of Housing, March 1971, pp. 119-21 for a discussion of the controversy surrounding the circular and the roles of NAHRO and NTO in its promulgation.

36. Sumpter vs. White Plains Housing Authority, Appellate Division, 1971. Cited in Journal of Housing, April 1971, unreasonable burden on the local authority.

37. Omaha Housing Authority vs. U. S. Housing Authority (HUD), 468 F.2d 8th Cir. 1972.

38. George Shermer, Housing is the Tenants, NAHRO (Washington, D.C.: U.S. Government Printing Office, 1967), pp. 37-40.

39. George Shermer, More than Shelter, op. cit., pp. 31, 84.

40. Ibid., p. 92.

41. Edward Banfield, The Unheavenly City: The Nature and Future of Our Urban Crisis (Boston: Little, Brown and Co., 1968).

42. Roger Starr, "Which of the Poor Shall Live in Public Housing," The Public Interest, Spring 1971, pp. 116-24.

43. Ibid., pp. 117-18.

44. William Gamson, Power and Discontent (Homewood, Ill.: The Dorsey Press, 1968).

2

TWO DECADES OF EXPLANATIONS—
AND SOME HYPOTHESES

Attempts to explain the existence of problem tenants through the years have all flowed from a preoccupation with the unique traits that presumably characterize them. These are all, regardless of the causative processes they stress, referred to here as "individual pathology explanations." This chapter reviews several of the explanations of this type that have been particularly influential in the thinking of housing and social welfare professionals who have been active in seeking answers to the problem of the problem tenant.

In this discussion it is the "multi-problem family" that occupies center stage, the assumption having been that it was primarily this phenomenon that constituted management's problem tenants. The multi-problem family was first looked at statistically, then defined functionally, then analyzed psychologically, and subsequently explained sociologically and culturally; but the focus remained upon these presumably special kinds of families. Thus, although many commentators concentrated upon issues of class or culture, it was primarily to describe the genesis of those same families whose unique characteristics remained the basis for the individual pathology explanation of problem tenants.

Having reviewed the traditional position in its many disguises, we shall then move, with the welcome assistance of the Chicago school's labeling theory, toward an alternative explanation of problem-tenant identification, which is referred to in this study as the "interactive" theory. This proposition, along with a physical design correlate, is then formulated in a series of testable hypotheses.

THE INDIVIDUAL PATHOLOGY EXPLANATION

That the unique characteristics of individual families were seized upon as the probable explanation of management's problems with its tenants is understandable. There are, in real life, particular families whose style, patterns of behavior, and child-rearing and housekeeping practices are simply so unusual (in contrast to the style, patterns, and practices of their neighbors) that they stand out.

The Multi-Problem Family Discovered

Systematic attempts to identify and classify these families seem to have begun shortly after World War II, with the Bradley Buell study in St. Paul in 1948 representing a real bench mark.[1] In a sense, the multi-problem family was "discovered" in this much discussed survey, which revealed between two and three percent of the families to be absorbing over one-half of the health and welfare services, and representing a disproportionate share of the deviant behavior. In the St. Paul study multi-problem families were defined as families with one or more children under 18 years of age with serious behavior disorders, emotional disturbances, severe conflicts in interpersonal relations; and problems in economic functioning and health.

This survey, and the many that followed it, relied entirely upon the judgments of therapeutic health and welfare agencies in the assignment of multi-problem status to individual families. They assumed that (1) all or most of the families meeting the criteria had had contacts with these agencies and that the identified families represented a true reflection of their actual proportion in the community, and (2) that there was a high degree of internal consistency among the judges participating in the survey. Although their methodology was entirely reliant upon a family's having come to the attention of the community, the nature of this interaction was not considered to be central to the identification process.

Subsequent studies in Vancouver, New Haven, and elsewhere repeated the survey technique; and, in spite of problems of spotty reporting and frequent disagreement among agencies, they confirmed the existence of two to three percent multi-problem families.[2] In one public housing neighborhood in New Haven the combined judgment of the social agencies surveyed revealed a high eight percent, a figure that reappeared at housing conferences for a decade.[3] Quite naturally, as a partial result of this process of assigning the multi-problem label, the conviction that these families were qualitatively different and uniquely pathological became widespread.

A Functional Approach to the Multi-Problem Family

One of those involved in the St. Paul work went on to lead subsequent studies into the characteristics of multi-problem families.

L. Geismar sought a more sophisticated functional definition of the multi-problem family, and his publication in 1964 of Understanding the Multi-Problem Family[4] was widely read in housing circles. Geismar's objectives were true to the traditions of applied social science in that he was interested not only in (1) the definition and identification of multi-problem families, (2) the description and measurement of degrees of malfunction, and (3) the identification of conditions associated with the malfunctioning, but also in (4) the implications for diagnosis, treatment, and community services.[5] It may be that this eagerness to have his findings be useful for the practitioner of existing professions influenced his perspective in such a way that he concentrated heavily upon the intrafamilial functioning of his subject and tended to reinforce, among persons dealing with tenant problems in public housing, the individual pathology explanation of most difficulties.

Geismar's definition of the multi-problem family was:

a family with disorganized social functioning of an order that adversely affects the following sets of behavior: (1) relationships inside the family; (2) relationships outside the family group; particularly neighborhood and community relations; and (3) the performance of tasks such as those concerned with health and with economic and household practices that are designed to maintain the family as a physical unit. Not just a family with problems—rather a permanent or repeated breakdown in performance of basic functions.[6]

In his functional description of family problems he refers to the work of Parsons and Bales, Family Socialization and Interaction Process,[7] with its emphasis on the roles of family members in their internal activities and their relationships to other social systems. It is Geismar's concept of the family as a system or "aggregate of interdependent parts with an underlying degree of organization" relative to "more or less clearly or vaguely defined goals"[8] that leads him to stress the disorganized quality of his subject families.

Geismar attempted to soften the distinction between multi-problem and normal families by developing a three-part typology of "inadequate," "marginal," and "adequate," with scores assigned in each of 26 functioning categories that were themselves divided between intrafamilial and extrafamilial and between those characterized by social (expressive) and those by instrumental goals. By plotting the mean scores of each family type he discovered that the greatest difference between inadequate and adequate families was in those functional categories that were both intrafamilial and expressive (such as "individual behavior and adjustment," style of "care and training of children," "family relations and unity"), rather than those that were more utilitarian or instrumental and extra-familial.[9]

In searching for predictive variables, Geismar found that those categories of functioning that were most easily observable (such as household conditions, health conditions, and practices, economic practices, use of community resources) were the least indicative of an inadequately functioning family in the terms of their entire 26 category range. Since it is these more public, extrafamilial categories that would make it likely that a family would come to the attention of its neighbors and of the management of its apartment house, and since it was in these categories that there was least difference between the multi-problem families and the others, it follows that the multi-problem families would not be expected to account for a disproportionate share of the tenant problems. At least it should have.

This point was somehow lost in the rush to apply Geismar's insights in programs of treatment. Concerned with the full range of family functioning, finding the intra-familial expressive functioning to be most in need of repair, and already committed to the effectiveness of intensive casework in helping such families, he called for aggressive family casework on a grand scale.[10]

Other Individual Pathology Theories

While Geismar concentrated on the relative disorganization of the functioning of family units, he did not attempt to develop an elaborate theory of causation. Others equally committed to the individual pathology explanation have done so, basing their work largely on the intrapsychic theories that have grown out of the psychoanalytic movement. A recent example may be found in the writings of Eleanor Pavenstedt and her associates in a longitudinal study of children of "disorganized lower-class families."[11]

In her study of "disorganized, maximally deprived families," Dr. Pavenstedt found support for three hypotheses:

1. In order to lead out of misery, as well as out of intellectual dearth, intervention must begin very early and be concerned with total personality development.
2. Only by supporting overall developmental maturation can children be helped to attain the personality and cognitive tools with which to build satisfactory lives for themselves.
3. The children's early experiences are the most decisive influences in the perpetuation of the maladaption of these families over generations.[12]

By chance, she was simultaneously involved in another project with the children from stable working-class families in the same part of Boston and able to observe a pronounced contrast. She characterized the disorganized families and their members as being in a state of "drift," ridden by impulses, unable to defer gratification or to modify aggression, and generally distrustful and suspicious of others. For both the children and their mothers the boundaries of the self were fluid and characterized by oscillating identity themes— a "plurality of inconsistent identities." Because these families were in a state of chronic crisis, their contacts with community agencies were multiple. When they did live in public housing developments they were well known to the management.

The Pavenstedt diagnosis is one of children being raised by mothers who were themselves badly deprived as infants, still seeking infantile needs on a level "hardly more advanced than their children," and "lacking in the minimal elements of internal organization and motivation." The families she studied would occupy the extreme end of the Geismar family functioning scale but would undoubtedly have had very low scores not only in the expressive intrafamilial categories but also in the extrafamilial areas where the average multi-problem family did not vary greatly from his adequately functioning neighbors.

While she rejected the then new concept of a "culture of poverty" (this is interesting in view of Edward Banfield's affection for her work), she did see the problems of the "drifters" as being passed on from generation to generation via extreme maternal deprivation, through psychological rather than either social or cultural processes. She felt that intensive casework would be helpful but that it should be buttressed by an array of other supportive services for the mothers and by early intensive relationships for the children with other adults who could provide what the mothers could not. Preschool nursery schools were one mechanism through which this might be done.

CLASS AND CULTURAL DETERMINANTS WITHIN
THE TRADITIONAL FRAMEWORK

In their discussions of the multi-problem family neither Geismar nor Pavenstedt suggested that this was an exclusively lower-class phenomenon, although Pavenstedt's subjects were so severely disorganized it would probably have been difficult for them to retain any higher class identification. Other writers have, on the contrary, viewed the multi-problem family as an exclusively lower-class characteristic, in some cases its most important defining feature.

Walter Miller is perhaps the most articulate spokesman for this position, seeing multi-problem families not as suffering from a deprivation-based pathology, or even functioning on an inadequate disorganized level, but rather as the "normative actor," virtually the standard bearer, of the lower class.[13] Many of the characteristics identified by others as the product of psychological factors he sees as "features of a complex and ramified style of life whose component characteristics . . . evince an order of mutual coherence that . . . derives from the particular and complicated role played by the low-skilled laboring population with respect to the total social and economic order."[14] What others see as disorganization and pathology fitting for treatment and rehabilitation strategies he sees as a natural and internally organized life style—a product of our stratified social order.

While exponents of individual pathology explanations of multi-problem families suggested therapy and social services, and Walter Miller suggested, rather, that they be left alone, perhaps the most popular view of the 1960s was that they should be educated. This strategy and its underlying theory, that of the "culture of poverty," emerged, ironically, out of the same political-social event that also gave rise to its severest critics: the "war on poverty" of the middle 1960s.

The anthropologist whose name is most often associated with the concept of the culture of poverty was Oscar Lewis. He believed that he had found, in observational studies in several different cultures, a subculture of poverty that transcended regional, rural, urban, and national differences. Lewis saw what he described as "remarkable cross-national similarities in family structure, interpersonal relations, time orientation, value systems, and spending patterns" among the poor[15] and argued that this represented not merely a like collection of isolated traits based in economic deprivation but an integrated cluster of traits that constituted a culture.

These grouped traits (among them the lack of effective participation in the major institutions of larger society, low literacy, awareness of but lack of commitment to middle-class values, maternal deprivation, absence of a prolonged childhood, and inability to defer gratification) represent, in Lewis' view, "both an adaptation and reaction of the poor to their marginal position in a class-stratified, highly individuated, capitalistic society."[16] He argued that the culture of poverty does not arise in primitive societies and declines in socialist ones. It is a culture that, like all cultures, provides men with "a design for living, with a ready-made set of solutions for human problems," and once established it tends to be transmitted from generation to generation.[17]

If multi-problem families were not necessarily pathological but rather carriers of a distinctive culture of poverty, then it was clear that the self-perpetuating nature of the problem could best be affected by programs of education and "cultural enrichment." It was not long, however, before a counter-movement arose that detected a pejorative aspect of the culture of poverty theory: namely, the implication that the cause of poverty and its associated traits of individual behavior were somehow lodged in the poor themselves. A great debate was soon underway over the validity of the culture of poverty concept;[18] and, although Lewis argued to the end that "there is nothing in the concept that puts the onus of poverty on the character of the poor,"[19] the culture of poverty as an explanation of the traits associated with poverty and with multi-problem families in particular had fallen from favor.

OTHER PERSPECTIVES ON INDIVIDUAL PATHOLOGY

Thus in the course of less than twenty years, a period of intense activity in the social sciences and social reform, a variety of artic-ulately stated explanations were offered to account for the range of human difficulties that seemed prevalent in low-income neighbor-hoods and, particularly, in public housing developments. All focused primarily on the individual families themselves, though in terms of several different processes. Managers of housing developments and directors of housing programs tried to keep up with the theories. They were told on one hand that their difficulties with their tenants were caused by the presence of a small number of multi-problem families that needed at least some good casework to help them to improve their level of functioning and, in some cases, in-depth therapy for the parents and parent-surrogate arrangements for the children. On the other hand, they were told on equally good authority that their tenants were locked into lower-class cultural patterns and were un-likely to respond to programs aimed at changing them and should be ignored or isolated. Finally, in the midst of great national upheaval, they are told that their tenants are culturally deprived and in need of training and education, and no sooner have they incorporated this concept than they are informed that those traits that have been de-scribed by so many diverse scholars are not really the product of cultural transfer between generations but of dynamic adaptation to societal deprivation. Given such a choice of legitimated views, managers have understandably been hard pressed to find a personal orientation and style that would be at once compatible with the wide range of learned opinions available, the personal characteristics they bring to the job, and the unique social properties and reputation of the development in which they work.

22

As the day-to-day activity of housing management proceeds, however, some families continue to emerge as problem tenants; and while the explanations of their presumed deviance (Geismar, Pavenstedt, and Miller all drew heavily from public housing populations) continue to be applied with limited success,other processes are clearly at work. Managers are interacting with tenants and tenants with other tenants, and all of this within the context of the development's reputation in the collective perceptions of staff, tenants, and community. All of the players in this interaction enter the stage with a certain set of expectations, and these expectations may have some effect on what happens next.

This perspective involves a whole new set of forces and the distinct possibility that a scapegoating process may be at work here, both within a development with regard to certain families and within a community with regard to certain developments. Unfortunately the analyses already cited have little to contribute to this line of inquiry, and for assistance we must look elsewhere in social theory.

A BREAK WITH TRADITION: LABELING THEORY

In none of the writings discussed above was it seriously doubted that the roots of the problem-tenant phenomenon can be found in pathological or aberrant processes of either psychic, social, or cultural origin. Alternative explanations that might have focused on the importance of the interaction of families upon one another or the effect of selected social variables have received little or no discussion, either in housing-management or scholarly circles. This is surprising in that there are other well-established theories in the social science literature that might suggest approaches quite unlike the more popular ones already reviewed.

One theory that offers a particularly promising format for the analysis of "deviancy" of all types (and the problem tenant has certainly been viewed as deviant by housing management and, in many cases, by the neighboring community) has focused on the process by which a label of deviant is assigned to an individual family or group and the effect that the labeling itself then has upon the subsequent behavior of the person labeled.

The study of the labeling process, the core of the deviancy theory of the so-called Chicago school of sociology, represents a significant break with the more generally accepted attempts at explaining problems of all kinds in terms of factors within the offending individual. The deviancy theorists, particularly Howard Becker, Edwin Lemert, Erving Goffman, and, more recently, Thomas Scheff, have concentrated instead upon the interaction between the potentially

23

deviant individual and the labeling community or group. The thinking
of these theorists may provide a basis on which to develop an alternative "interactional" approach to the study of problem tenants in
public housing.

It was Becker's view that groups, not individuals, created
deviance "by making the rules whose infraction constitutes deviance,
and by applying those rules to particular people and labeling them
as outsiders."[20] Many rules are broken, but for the rule breaker
to be singled out he must first be caught by someone and, second,
someone must take some step to enforce the rule. Thus before the
rule-breaking tenant can be identified as a problem tenant someone
must first observe his behavior and then object strongly enough to
it to bring it to the attention of a larger group or of the rule-enforcing
authorities.

Goffman then explored the mechanisms through which those
applying the labels go about making them stick. Society, he pointed
out, establishes ways of "categorizing persons and the complement
of attitudes felt to be ordinary and natural for members of each of
these categories."[21] Thus we are able to anticipate the attitudes
and behaviors of persons we have categorized. Further, we "lean
on these anticipations . . . transforming them into . . . righteously
presented demands," and in the force of such pressure from the
majority the labeled persons tend to comply.

Scheff built on Becker and Goffman's analysis by developing
a social-system model of how deviant behavior becomes stabilized:[22]
the critical point in the process was the instant at which a primary,
experimental, or even random deviant action is identified and publicly
labeled. From this point onward the label itself becomes a major
factor, reinforced by group pressure and official action, and finally
incorporated by the deviant himself as a part of his self-identity.
As Lemert has said, it gets "inside the skin" of the deviant.[23] Scheff
pointed out that everyone indulges in some "residual rule-breaking,"
but most of it is undetected and unrecorded and doesn't lead to anything that might be considered a "deviant career." On the other hand,
once a public crisis occurs, involving public labeling of the residual
rule breaking as deviance (such as mental illness, criminality, per-
version), the labeling group begins to relate to the labeled party in
ways that amplify the deviant role.

Certainly if this process is at work in the identification of problem tenants it exists in an attenuated form. Only rarely, as in the
case of the occasional tenant who becomes the subject of eviction
proceedings for causes other than nonpayment of rent, is a tenant
so definitively labeled as the mental patient, criminal, or other
deviants studied by the Chicago theorists. Nevertheless, the dynamic
view of the labeling process that they have developed may be applicable

to (1) the "career" of the problem tenant who, once identified via a complaint by a neighbor to the management, may pass over the line from normal tenant to the status of problem (deviant) tenant; or (2) the "career of a development" that, once labeled as a problem project, may be subject to processes that tend to reinforce that reputation.

Once cast in the role of problem tenant, a resident may find himself playing this part, albeit reluctantly, in his immediate neighborhood and vis-à-vis management. As Lemert has pointed out, this may be a very important, though painful, function: the scapegoat draws to himself aggression and blame for a range of social and psychological problems in the group, thus strengthening feelings of homogeneity and consensus among other group members.[24] From what is known of the prevalence of scapegoating in public housing projects[25] we might assume that many problem tenants are identified as a result of just such a process.

Similarly, while a label affixed to a specific family may then play an important role in the subsequent career of that family, a label affixed to a whole category of families (as in the multi-problem family or the dependent family) or to an entire housing development (in the form of a negative reputation) may play an equally important role in the subsequent career of that category or that development. By establishing a set of mutual expectations that are held in common by most of the players, be they management staff, tenants, or members of the community at large, it is possible that these expectations in turn influence the behavior of all interacting participants.

In developments that enjoy a high reputation in the community a tenant will probably approach his neighbors and be approached by them in an atmosphere of positive expectations. Expecting one's neighbors to be "nice" may thus increase the probability that the resulting interaction will be characterized by niceness. A manager expecting niceness from the tenants in his high-reputation development may be more likely to minimize the negative aspects of interactions that do take place.

In like manner, both tenants and managers occupying a housing development that has a poor reputation in the community may all approach the situation with negative expectations that, by coloring the subsequent interactions, tend to confirm the negative conclusions about the character of the development. If this process is significantly influential it may produce the classic self-fulfilling prophecy, with both labeled groups of tenants and developments easy targets for scapegoating by managers, other tenants, and the spokesmen for the community at large (such as the mass media, public officials, and civic leaders).

FAMILY INTERACTION AS A FACTOR IN
PROBLEM-TENANT IDENTIFICATION

Building on the conceptual base established by the labeling theorists, it may be possible to develop an alternative theory to explain the identification of problem tenants; a theory that relies more heavily on the interaction among tenants than upon their individual characteristics. The remainder of this chapter addresses this goal.

People interact, in neighborhoods and communities, in ways that are partly determined by their likeness or unlikeness. Thus, while some observers have lauded the heterogeneous community as preferable to any of a variety of segregated living arrangements,[26] others have noted that heterogeneity of class, lifestyle, age, and other variables may, in addition to adding "spice" to the neighborhood, also contribute a great deal of the conflict, fear, and discord. Gans' description of the clash between working- and middle-class residents in Levittown over such items as child rearing practices, priorities for public expenditures, and style of education is one illustration.[27] Similarly, Wilson's discussion of the "urban unease" and the preoccupation of many city dwellers with "crime in the streets" lays much of this to the close proximity of diverse social classes with divergent notions of what kind of behavior is appropriate in public places.[28]

Class, however, is an elusive concept, especially when dealing with an entirely low-income public-housing population in which class distinctions would have to be based on less measurable factors. Class differences in lifestyle may indeed be the basis of much of the intertenant conflict in a given housing development, but the difficulty of establishing this through widespread and intimate observation takes it beyond the resources of this study. Establishing class on the basis of available socioeconomic data would be out of the question because the population does not vary significantly in either income or employment, the two most generally recognized criteria for the assignment of class. If "unlikeness" is an important determinant of interfamily interaction among the tenants, then data on variables other than social class will have to be the subject of examination.

There are more precise variables available that may play just as important a part in the generation of conflict between tenants. For example, Irving Rosow's study of the social integration of the aged offers strong evidence of the effect of the residential concentration of aged people in an apartment house upon the extent of interaction between neighbors.[29] If, as Rosow found, interaction with neighbors increases as more of one's neighbors are of one's own age, then it might be equally true that the quality of neighborliness would deteriorate as more of one's neighbors are of a different age.

Similarly, one might speculate over the impact of like or unlike family sizes, or ages of children, or the sex of the head of household, upon the quality of the interaction between neighbors, and upon the incidence of complaints to the management and the subsequent labeling of a problem tenant.

The effect of the composition of a given group upon the quality of the interaction as well as on the nature of commonly held attitudes has been the subject of considerable investigation in other settings. The "American Soldier" studies of the importance of reference groups upon individual attitudes and behavior represent some of the earliest efforts in a like area.[30] More recent attempts to analyze the effect of group composition have included those by James Davis[31] and Arnold Tannenbaum,[32] who dealt primarily with the methodological difficulties of separating structural from individual effects, and the Kriesberg study of low-income families in several Syracuse housing development neighborhoods.[33] Most of these studies dealt with neighborhood-wide characteristics through the analysis of fairly large groups of data gathered through extensive interviewing. They did not attempt to face the microscale differences within, say, a given apartment building or stairhall. Yet it is this level with which we are now concerned.

There is some evidence that there are certain family types that, in the abstract, represent potentially threatening neighbors for large numbers of housing tenants. Morton Isler, in the preliminary findings of a study that spanned both public and private housing developments, notes that when asked what kinds of neighbors they preferred most tenants showed some distinct preferences.[34] For instance, less than 10 percent preferred a family with children in which both parents worked, unsupervised children representing a serious problem in many developments. Given a choice between a widow with children and a divorcee with children, most felt it made a difference and preferred the widow. On the other hand, variables such as race seemed less important, since more than two-thirds of the respondents in that study indicated no special concern about the color of their hypothetical neighbors. It may be that these firm preferences for certain family types over others are also reflected in the kinds of interaction between families who are already neighbors.

THE IMPORTANCE OF PHYSICAL DESIGN IN DETERMINING SOCIAL COMPOSITION

If, indeed, the social composition of a given apartment structure will have an effect upon the nature of the interaction between tenants there and, subsequently, upon the identification of problem tenants, it follows that architectural factors may frequently determine many of these compositional effects.

Most of the studies of the social impact of physical design have taken place over the past twenty years and have concentrated heavily upon the importance of propinquity in determining patterns of friendship groups. Leon Festinger's study of student housing in 1950,[35] followed by William Whyte's less rigorous study of Park Forest, Illinois,[36] established the importance of physical design upon the occurrence of chance meetings on which many friendships were based (at least in those communities). Although Gans and others later questioned the overemphasis upon this design factor (and the simultaneous neglect of such social factors as homogeneity of background, attitudes, and style),[37] the importance of design in setting the stage for subsequent interaction is generally accepted. Gans conceded that this was especially true when families were limited by financial factors in mobility, and when children were young (again limiting the mobility of many mothers), conditions which are present in the housing developments with which we are concerned.[38]

Such design factors as the density of large apartments, the juxtaposition of small apartments occupied by elderly or childless couples and those of large families, and the presence of elevators or courtyard culs-de-sac are likely to be instrumental in creating compositional situations that may yield greater or lesser incidence of conflict between neighbors. This, of course, is the other side of the Festinger proposition: if proximity is a determining factor in the establishment of amicable relationships then it is likely also to be a factor in the establishment of relationships that are basically incompatible.

SOME HYPOTHESES AND A GENERAL STRATEGY

This alternative explanation of the problem-tenant phenomenon can be formulated as a related set of hypotheses. The primary proposition of the alternative explanation is that families are problems to public housing managers because of the character of their interaction with immediate neighbors rather than by virtue of their particular social behaviors. A correlate to this is the proposition that certain design factors are instrumental in determining the social composition of apartment buildings and thus, to some extent, the interaction of families living there.

Families may become problems to management because of conflict with adjacent or nearby neighbors that arises as a result of incompatible demographic characteristics such as differences of age, family-cycle stage, or other factors; and, further, architectural design factors may be instrumental in influencing some of the compositional arrangements that in turn result in conflict between neighbors and their subsequent designation as problem tenants.

These general hypotheses suggest a range of specific questions that will need to be addressed. For example, is it true that a high concentration of large families in a single building is likely to result in a high level of interfamily conflict and a subsequent high number of problems for management? Conversely, does a design that instead places single bedroom units, likely to be occupied by the elderly, adjacent to large units create a conflict-prone situation? Do high-rise buildings seem to reduce conflict by increasing anonymity? Does a first-floor residence increase the chance of involvement in conflict? Is "dependency" really a determining factor in a family's becoming a problem to management? Is there evidence that conflict between neighbors is exacerbated by such factors as source of income, size of family, or whether the family is headed by a man or a woman? Is the age of the children in a family an important factor? These and other specific questions should be explored in research that addresses the broader propositions stated above.

Should the alternative explanation be supported by research evidence, implications for social policy would be numerous. Therapeutic programs instituted as a means of eliminating problems of families that have become problems to management would have to be reassessed. The importance of careful tenant placement would be underlined, with the possibility of a new set of previously over-looked criteria emerging—criteria that focus on the mix of families rather than upon the characteristics of the single applicant being assigned to an apartment. Finally, positive findings might have serious implications for the design of future family housing developments. Architects have received precious little assistance from social science in the past in dealing with the hard decisions of design, and this study will at least explore some questions with which men and women in the business of housing design must grapple daily.

Figure 2.1 illustrates the several populations that will be examined in this study.

In seeking an explanation of the problem-tenant phenomenon the study will first identify (A) the social characteristics of the entire population of selected public housing developments. It will then identify (B) those families that the managers consider to be problems and make comparisons of frequencies of social variables occurring in each of these two groups. Next it will examine the families involved in conflict with one another during a ten-week period: those complaining (D), and those being complained about (C). No attempt will be made to identify the parameters of (E), "multi-problem families."

Problem tenants (B) will then be studied to see the extent to which their social characteristics are related to the types of difficulties

FIGURE 2.1

Populations Under Investigation

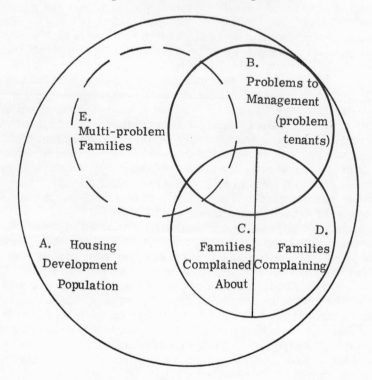

that have led them to be identified by their managers as problems. The families involved in conflict (C and D) will be examined to determine the association of their own social characteristics and the role they play in conflict episodes. Finally, the subject housing developments—selected to represent a range of community reputations as well as other characteristics—will be compared with one another in terms of the volume and type of problems uncovered, the quality of the intertenant conflict, and the importance of the social characteristics of the interacting tenants in that conflict.

In summary then, the traditional explanations of what creates the problem tenant have been based on the popular assumption that families troubling management are for the most part multi-problem or seriously deviant families, hence the emphasis on rehabilitation and therapeutic strategies in professional housing literature through the years. This study will first test the validity of this view by asking managers to identify the families in their tenant body that represent problems to them.

It will next explore the alternative explanation that it is the interaction among different types of families that creates problematic situations; incidents of complaints by one tenant against another will be monitored and analyzed. The investigation will seek information that will enable us to determine not only whether or not the alternative explanation is supportable but what specific factors may account for a significant proportion of problem circumstances and the architectural features that may have influenced their distribution.

The developments for study will be selected so as to represent the wide variety of disparate elements making up the entire population of housing developments rather than an "average" or "typical" set. Differences will be maximized, especially as they are expressed in a high or low community reputation. This will make it difficult to apply probability tests to the data when all of the sample developments are grouped unless the variables involved are similarly distributed in each. To this extent the study can be viewed as several substudies of distinct developments, except where the variables in question do not vary in frequency among developments.[39] Only by selecting our sample developments in this way can we emerge with some clue as to the differences between the manifestation of the problem family phenomenon in different types of developments and the association of community reputation with the difficulties managers are experiencing with their tenant populations.

Thus, in order to make meaningful comparisons between the problem tenants and the total population of the selected developments it will be necessary first to obtain fairly detailed base-line socio-economic data on the whole range of public housing tenants in a subject. Next a sample of housing developments reflecting differences of reputation and other social factors will have to be selected. Managers will then have to be interviewed so that they may identify those families whom they consider to be problems; and, finally, a complaint log will have to be kept for a suitable period of time on which incidents of tenant conflict reported to management will be recorded.

NOTES

1. Bradley Buell and Associates, Community Planning for Human Services (New York: Columbia University Press, 1952).
2. L. Geismar and M. LaSorte, Understanding the Multi-Problem Family (New York: Association Press, 1964), pp. 54-57.
3. Ibid., p. 58.
4. Ibid.

5. Ibid., pp. 12-13.
6. Ibid., pp. 35-36.
7. Talcott Parsons and Robert F. Bales, Family Socialization and Interaction Process (Glencoe, Illinois: The Free Press, 1955).
8. Geismar, op. cit., p. 37.
9. Ibid., p. 82.
10. Ibid., pp. 183-202.
11. Eleanor Pavenstedt, The Drifters; Children of Disorganized Lower-Class Families (Boston: Little, Brown and Co., 1967).
12. Ibid., pp. 5, 7.
13. Walter Miller, "The Elimination of the American Lower Class as National Policy," in D. P. Moynihan, ed., On Understanding Poverty (New York: Basic Books, 1968), pp. 260-315.
14. Ibid., p. 267.
15. Oscar Lewis, "The Culture of Poverty," in D. P. Moynihan, ed., On Understanding Poverty (New York: Basic Books, 1968), pp. 187-200.
16. Ibid.
17. Ibid., p. 197.
18. See Charles A. Valentine, Culture and Poverty—Critique and Counter Proposals, (Chicago: University of Chicago Press, 1968); Lee Rainwater and W. Yancey, The Moynihan Report and the Politics of Controversy (Cambridge: M.I.T. Press, 1967).
19. Lewis, op. cit., p. 199.
20. Howard S. Becker, The Outsiders; Studies in the Sociology of Deviance (Glencoe, Illinois: The Free Press, 1966), p. 9.
21. Erving Goffman, Stigma (Englewood Cliffs, N.J.: Prentice-Hall, 1963), p. 2.
22. Thomas J. Scheff, Being Mentally Ill: A Sociological Theory (Chicago: Aldine Publishing Co., 1966), p. 100.
23. Edwin Lemert, "Social Structure, Social Control, and Deviation," in E. Lemert, ed., Human Deviance, Social Problems and Social Control (Englewood Cliffs, N.J.: Prentice-Hall, 1967). pp. 16-17.
24. Edwin Lemert, "Paranoia and the Dynamics of Exclusion," in Lemert, op. cit., p. 209.
25. Lee Rainwater, "Fear and the House as Haven in the Lower Class," Journal of the American Institute of Planners 32 (1966): 23-37.
26. See the array of "antisuburban" writings beginning about 1950 and including William H. Whyte, The Organization Man (Garden City, N.J.: Doubleday, 1954); Harry Henderson, "The Mass-Produced Suburbs: How People Live in America's Newest Towns," Harper's, November 1953, pp. 25-32; David Riesman, The Lonely Crowd (New Haven: Yale University Press, 1950): Richard Sennett, "The Brutality of Modern Families," Transaction, September 1970.

27. Herbert J. Gans, The Levittowners (New York: Random House, 1967).

28. James Q. Wilson, "The Urban Unease," The Public Interest, Summer 1968, pp. 25-39.

29. Irving Rosow, Social Integration of the Aged (New York: Free Press, 1967).

30. S. A. Stauffer et al., Studies in Social Psychology in World War Two: The American Soldier During Army Life (Princeton, N.J.: Princeton University Press, 1949).

31. James A. Davis, Joe L. Spaeth, and Carolyn Huson, "A Technique for Analyzing the Effects of Group Composition," American Sociological Review, April 1961, pp. 215-25.

32. Arnold S. Tannenbaum, and Jerald G. Bachman, "Structural Versus Individual Effects," American Journal of Sociology, May 1964, pp. 585-95.

33. Louis Kriesberg, Mothers in Poverty: A Study of Fatherless Families (Chicago: Aldine Publishing Co., 1970).

34. Morton Isler, Housing Management: A Progress Report (Washington, D.C.: The Urban Institute, 1970) pp. 28-29.

35. Leon Festinger, Stanley Schacter, and Kurt Back, Social Pressures in Informal Groups, A Study of Human Factors in Housing (New York: Harper, 1950).

36. William H. Whyte, The Organization Man (Garden City, N.J.: Doubleday, 1957), pp. 372-77.

37. Herbert Gans, "Planning and Social Life," Journal of the American Institute of Planners, May 1961.

38. Ibid.

39. See the discussion of nonprobability sampling in Claire Seltiz, Marie Jahoda, Morton Deutsch, and Stuart Cook, Research Methods in Social Relations (New York: Holt, Rinehart and Winston, 1964), pp. 535-45.

3

HOUSING PROJECTS AND THEIR REPUTATIONS— PICKING SOME TARGETS

Because of its geographic proximity to Brandeis University and the openness and enthusiasm of key public officials, the public housing program in Boston, Massachusetts, was chosen as the setting for this research. At the time of writing the entire program consisted of 25 "family developments" occupied by families of all ages and sizes including elderly persons, and 15 "elderly" developments designed and constructed exclusively for the aged. In 1969 it housed 40,955 persons, representing 6.1 percent of the total Boston population.

HISTORY OF PUBLIC HOUSING IN BOSTON

This array of residential structures, dispersed throughout all sections of the city, did not arise full-blown but developed from a small beginning 36 years ago with the construction of the Old Harbor Village development in South Boston in 1935 (now renamed the Mary Ellen McCormack development). This 1,018-unit project was built under the auspices of the Public Works Administration, and in 1937 its management was assumed by the new Boston Housing Authority (BHA) created in response to the passage in Congress of the historic National Housing Act. The act provided for implementation through local housing authorities, and Boston duly established such an agency to manage the Old Harbor development and to expand that program. Old Harbor was followed quickly by projects in Charlestown, Roxbury (Mission Hill), the South End (Lenox Street), and South Boston (Old Colony), each now entering its thirtieth year of occupancy.

It was the end of the depression; and, with the Second World War on the horizon, the BHA saw itself as building primarily for the low-income but, nevertheless, stable working poor of that day. Except for the Lenox Street development, which had been built on cleared land in the black ghetto, the residents were almost exclusively white, married, and upwardly mobile.

During the war years the residents became heavily laced with war workers who merited priority in the tenant selection process. New developments were built in Roxbury (Orchard Park), East Boston (Maverick), and Jamaica Plain (Heath Street).

Shortly after the war the Commonwealth of Massachusetts enacted its own legislation to provide housing, particularly for veterans who had returned from their wartime duties to a discouragingly tight housing market. By the late 1940s and early 1950s "Veterans' Housing" under BHA auspices was going up in South Boston, the South End, Roslindale, Brighton, and elsewhere in the city. The residents of these developments were, once again, largely white, working- or middle-class, intact families who viewed public housing apartments as a temporary arrangement.

By then the United States Congress had passed the Housing Act of 1949, discussed briefly in Chapter 1. Because of the specific provisions of that act and the spirit with which it was implemented the housing construction it authorized was characterized by austerity of design, elevator buildings, high density, economy in the selection of sites, and a tenant population that was generally more needy, racially heterogeneous, and economically less mobile than previous tenant generations. The infamous monster projects of the mid-1950s— Columbia Point, Bromley Park, the Mission Hill Extension, and the South End's "Cathedral" project—were all products of this era.

No new family developments were built after 1954, in part because of the public revulsion toward the products of the previous period. It was only in the early 1960s, when the nation discovered its elderly to be a growing population group with acute housing problems, that the Congress created a special program for the construction of housing designed and built with the particular needs of the elderly in mind. This program was politically very popular, and several small, attractive, and much sought-after developments were constructed by the BHA in the mid-1960s.

DIVERSITY AMONG PROJECTS

The result of this history, then, is an array of developments that is far from uniform in size, style, background, or population. In fact, the program embraces great diversity—a reality that must be dealt with in any study pretending to address single aspects of the entire reality of public housing in Boston.

Although the Department of Housing and Urban Development (HUD) demands, as did its predecessor the Housing and Home Finance

Agency, that all local housing authorities conduct a yearly census and submit vast quantities of information to the Washington office, the data collected in these censuses has seen minimal use. Until the summer of 1970, when this writer conducted a social data analysis of the 1969 tenant census, the BHA had never taken a detailed look at the social and economic characteristics of its population.

The census itself, termed the Tenant Status Review (TSR), is carried out every year; but the elderly tenants (those heads of household over 62 years old in the federally assisted developments and 65 years old in those that are state assisted) are only interviewed every two years. Thus, the 1969 TSR data is the last total census now available in usable form as a base line for other research.[1]

The 1969 figures represent 13,295 interviews carried out by managers, assistant managers, and members of a special TSR team from the central BHA offices. Although they were conducted beginning in January, they all bear the official date of March 31, 1969, the date on which the census was completed.

The BHA population, as an aggregate, varies substantially from the population of the city of Boston at large. It is disproportionately both young and old, with relatively few non-elderly adults, especially males, in most developments. While school-age children represent 12 percent of the Boston population, they make up 26 percent of the BHA tenant population,[2] and, while the total BHA population makes up only 6.1 percent of Boston, the BHA's elementary-school-age children represent 13.8 percent of the 76,400 children of this age in the city as a whole.

The high proportion of elderly residents is especially impressive. Whereas 27.4 percent of the heads of families are over sixty years of age citywide,[3] in the BHA housing developments this proportion reaches 40 percent, ranging widely between developments.

As might be expected, the BHA family income profile is considerably lower than that of the city at large. The modal point for BHA family incomes falls within the $2,000-2,900 range, with a mean family income of $3,667. Forty percent of the BHA families have incomes of less than $3,000, while in the City of Boston only 15.7 percent of the families fall into the same category.[4] The number of families with incomes above $10,000 is relatively small—less than 2 percent of the entire tenant population.

The source of this income is mixed, with a large proportion receiving all of their income from sources other than employment. Sixty-eight percent of the BHA families have no employed adults as compared to 24.4 percent for the city at large.[5] In 1965, only four years before the 1969 TSR, 51.5 percent of the families had had no working member, indicating a 32 percent increase in dependency upon public assistance and other transfer programs in just four years.

In 1969, 45 percent of BHA families were receiving some sort of public assistance (not including OASDI or Veterans' benefits); 27 percent were on Aid to Families with Dependent Children (AFDC); 14 percent on Old Age Assistance (OAA); and 4 percent on Aid to the Permanently and Totally Disabled (APTD). This compares with a citywide picture in which only 19 percent of the households are receiving public assistance: 10 percent on AFDC, 6 percent on OAA, and .02 percent on APTD.

While the city of Boston includes about 17 percent nonwhite families, nonwhites represent 32 percent of the units under BHA management. The bulk of these nonwhite families are housed in predominantly black developments in spite of a concerted BHA effort in the mid-1960s to desegregate its formerly all-white family projects.

In terms of population stability, the BHA developments are experiencing a relatively high turnover rate, with 43 percent of the tenants having been in residence only five years or less. This compares unfavorably with the citywide average of 24.2 percent for the same duration of residence.[6] As is true with all of these variables, there is great variation among developments, some becoming more stable with time and others becoming less so. In some developments over 50 percent of the families have been in occupancy for 5 years or less, while others have up to 14 percent with more than 26 years of residence.

In family size the distribution of the BHA tenant population is not remarkable, with the exception of the larger proportion of one-person families than might be found in the city as a whole (BHA 33 percent to 23.9 percent citywide). Although there is a somewhat larger than usual number of family units with eight or more persons (6 percent BHA to 3.1 percent citywide), the popular image of the housing development overrun with oversized families is decidedly false. On the contrary, what characterizes many developments is the high proportion of small, elderly-headed families and a relative scarcity of families headed by persons between 40 and 60 years of age. While this is the picture in several developments, at the opposite end of the spectrum there are several projects with extremely high percentages of family heads under 30 years of age, one with 32 percent while the comparable citywide figure is only 20 percent.

Together with the large number of elderly, another factor that distinguishes the BHA tenant population from the rest of the city is the high proportion of single parent families. In six developments, over 50 percent of the non-elderly families are headed by a single parent, leaving these neighborhoods with a non-elderly adult-male-to-child ratio as low as one-to-ten.

All of these observations have applied to the public housing program as a whole. Unfortunately, similar profiles made up entirely of arithmetic means have been used in the past to portray public-housing developments and their residents in terms of monolithic over-simplification, and a myth of the typical project has been created in the public mind. In fact, there is great variation among developments not only in their physical design but in the distribution of social and economic variables within their populations. To illustrate this diversity, Table 3.1 records both the mean and the range of frequencies of occurrence of several key variables as observed in the twenty-five family developments.

There is a vast difference among individual developments not only in terms of specific variables but also in the way in which they are perceived by their own residents and by the inhabitants of the neighborhoods that surround them. Just one example of this is found in Gerald Taube's study of the contrast found between two developments in just one neighborhood, South Boston.[7] Concentrating on the Mary Ellen McCormack (previously Old Harbor Village) development and the state-assisted project known as the West Broadway, or D Street project, Taube showed how dramatically different the developments are, although similar in size, racial or ethnic composition, and general economic status. McCormack, although physically older, is in markedly better condition, enjoys higher status in the community,

TABLE 3.1

Selected Population Characteristics: Boston
Housing Authority Tenants, 1969
(in percentages)

	Average, All Projects	Range of Averages of Individual Projects
Age: head over 60	40	7—59
Dependency:		
families on AFDC	27	5—55
families with no		
employed member	68	20—77
Race: nonwhite families	32	1—100
Transiency: families with		
5 or fewer years occupancy	43	24—68
Family structure: single-		
parent families	44	20—68

38

suffers less from vandalism, vacancies, or stigmatization in the public press. Similar contrasts can be found among different developments in other parts of the city.

As noted in Chapter 2, some developments are believed by most persons who are aware of the whole range of projects to be more desirable as a place for families to live than are others. The reputation of a development thus appears to be an important variable to consider when attempting to make differential judgments regarding one development in relation to any of the others.

In selecting developments for study as part of this research it was crucial that we be able to differentiate among developments with more precision than would be possible through a simple comparison of available social and economic statistics. The phenomenon of reputation would have to be addressed if subject developments truly reflecting the diversity within the overall program could be selected. The following section deals with the problem of preparation for the selection of target areas.

REPUTATION AS AN INDEPENDENT VARIABLE

In attempting to isolate the phenomenon of reputation for more precise examination it is valuable to view it, initially, as an independent, discrete variable that can be defined operationally and, if possible, reduced to a set of interval scores amenable to statistical analysis. Once this is done it should be possible to examine the extent to which reputation correlates with other pertinent social and economic variables and, perhaps, to suggest interdependent relationships that may exist among variables.

The Reputational Scale was constructed in the following manner. Four "judges" were selected from the central office staff of the BHA. Each had intimate knowledge of all of the developments. Three of the judges were white; one was black. They represented the following positions at the Authority: director of management, chief of tenant selection, chief of social planning, and director of public information. Each judge was given a list of developments and asked to assign a score from one to seven for each development, where one represents very high and seven very low in a development's "physical desirability in relation to all of the other developments." Specific reference to the "physical desirability" was made in order to avoid having the racial composition of any development influence the more general judgment regarding desirability. The scores given by the four judges for each development were averaged and tested for reliability using Cronbach's "alpha," which yielded a coefficient of .52, indicating an acceptable level of internal consistency within the scale.[8] Reputation scores ranged from a high of 1.25 to a low of 6.50, with a mean score of 3.7.

Next, to identify those variables that are consistently associated with the community standing of a project as reflected in its Reputation Score,correlation coefficients were calculated based on frequencies of social and economic variables obtained from the 1969 TSR and from management records on such factors as vacancy rates and rent arrears. While this exercise could not hope to explore causative relationships, it did aim at: (1) clarifying the factors that may influence or be associated with community attitudes reflected in a project's reputation; (2) identifying dimensions along which developments truly differ in order to assist in the selection of unlike developments for further study and comparison. Correlations were obtained using the Data-Text program on an IBM #7094 computer. [9]

The following variables were included in the resulting correlation matrix (see Table 3.2): (1) size of development (in number of apartment units); (2) per capita income; (3) ratio of children to adult, non-elderly males; (4) percentage of nonwhite families; (5) age of development (years since initial occupancy); (6) percent of heads of households over 60 years of age; (7) percent of households with no employed workers; (8) percent of households on AFDC; (9) percent of households in occupancy five years or less; (10) percent of heads of household under 30 years of age; (11) percent of units vacated during year; (12) percent of households two months or more in arrears in rent; and (14) reputation score.

In addition to obtaining correlation coefficients (Pearson's Product Moment), each variable was converted into nominal categories (high and low) in order to better illustrate, as crosstabulations (Tables 3.3-3.9), the relationships already identified in the correlation matrix. In the creation of these crosstabulation tables, each variable was divided at the mean rather than at the midpoint of the range in order to eliminate the effect of extreme skewness in some variables.

It is clear at the outset that there are several mutually dependent variables that will, because of their structural relationship, be quite highly correlated with one another. These fall into three groups:

The "child factor" group: adult non-elderly males to child ratios AFDC percentage; single-parent families; and heads under 30 years of age.

Income: the high correlation with age 60 or above and the negative correlation with heads under 30 is a result of the per capita basis of the income figures. (An elderly individual or couple will usually have a higher per capita income than the individual members of a large family with children.)

40

TABLE 3.2

Boston Housing Authority, 1969: Correlation Coefficients, for Selected Variables

	1	2	3	4	5	6	7	8	9	10	11	12	13	14
1 Development size	1.000	-.245	.173	-.206	.363	.326	.433[a]	.154	-.084	.034	.13	.128	.349	.324
2 Per capita income		1.000	-.718[b]	-.047	.295	.425[a]	-.457[a]	-.785[b]	-.629[b]	-.732[b]	-.655[b]	-.549[b]	-.691[b]	-.720[b]
3 Child: Adult non-elderly male			1.000	.511[b]	-.295	-.328	.553[b]	.888[b]	.464[a]	.711[b]	.663[b]	.779[b]	.649[b]	.806[b]
4 Percent nonwhite				1.000	-.041	-.219	.310	.562[b]	.139	.374	.168	.608[b]	.207	.453[a]
5 Development age					1.000	.436[a]	.208	-.171	-.202	-.189	-.200	-.022	.051	-.067
6 Percent heads over 60 years						1.000	.427[a]	-.441[a]	-.348	-.650[b]	-.142	-.191	-.240	-.103
7 Percent no workers							1.000	.590[b]	.324	.228	.550[b]	.669[b]	.530[b]	.783[b]
8 Percent AFDC								1.000	.600[b]	.840[b]	.675[b]	.804[b]	.693[b]	.843[b]
9 Percent 5 years occupancy or less									1.000	.710[b]	.819[b]	.399[b]	.558[b]	.618[b]
10 Percent heads under 30										1.000	.659[b]	.527[b]	.668[b]	.652[b]
11 Percent vacant apartments											1.000	.500[a]	.755[b]	.815[b]
12 Percent single-parent families												1.000	.546[b]	.729[b]
13 Percent 2 months in arrears													1.000	.846[b]
14 Reputation score														1.000

[a] Significant at .05 level.
[b] Significant at .01 level.

Note: N = 25 housing developments.

41

Transiency: vacated apartments, occupancy of five years or less.

High correlations among the variables within these three groups are therefore less significant than their coefficients might indicate.

Bearing this in mind, the following observations are made regarding specific findings of interest:

There is no correlation of the size of the development with any other variable. One might have expected that the very large developments might have correlated negatively with reputation, but they did not. (See Table 3.2.)

Nonwhite race correlated highly with single-parent families as might have been expected. What is interesting is that it did not correlate with families with no workers or occupancy of five years or less (much has been made of the recent influx of black families, which has apparently been less remarkable than popularly reported) and yielded a very low correlation with reputation. (See Tables 3.2 and 3.3.)

Five years or less in occupancy is highly correlated with both the child factor group and with the reputation of the development, indicating a close relationship between these three factors: child density, transiency, and reputation. (See Tables 3.2 and 3.4).

Reputation appears to be associated closely with variables indicating high density of children, high transiency, and economic dependency. (See Tables 3.2, 3.5, 3.6, and 3.7.) Only two out of the twenty-five developments were able to achieve a high reputation score with a high ratio of children to non-elderly adult males. In no case was a development with a high number of nonworkers or of vacancies able to achieve a high reputation. When the development is serving as shelter to those families in the community who are most vulnerable in terms of being youthful, newly formed, or newly broken, of a discriminated minority, and so on, who are in effect the prime target group of the public housing program, it is likely to suffer a poor reputation for its troubles.

Thus there are certain variables regarding child density, transiency, and economic dependency that are related statistically, at a high level of significance (.001). These are the same factors that relate significantly to problems in management such as rent arrears and to the formation of negative community attitudes toward the developments.

This information is particularly helpful in selecting developments for further study and comparison. It indicates that it would not be useful to select them in terms of either their scale (size) or the racial composition of the tenant population. Rather, it suggests that if we are seeking to emphasize the differences among developments in our analysis, greater emphasis should be placed upon

TABLE 3.3

Crosstabulation: Reputation by Race

		Reputation Score		Total	Percent
		High	Low		
Nonwhite	Low	71.4	54.5		
		10	6	16	64.0
	High	28.6	45.5		
		4	5	9	36.0
Total		14	11	25	
Percent		56.0	44.0		100.0

Note: X^2 = 11.402. Not significant, with 1 df.

TABLE 3.4

Crosstabulation: Reputation by Length of Occupancy

		Reputation Score		Total	Percent
		High	Low		
Percent five years occupancy or less	Low	92.9	27.3		
		13	3	16	64.0
	High	7.1	72.7		36.0
		1	8	9	
Total		14	11	25	
Percent		56.0	44.0		100.0

Note: X^2 = 11.500. Significant at p = 0.001, with 1 df.

TABLE 3.5

Crosstabulation: Reputation by Ratio of Children to Non-elderly Adult Males

| | | Reputation Score | | Total | Percent |
		High	Low		
		85.7	18.2		
	Low				
		12	2	14	56.0
Children per non-elderly adult male					
		14.3	81.8		
	High				
		2	9	11	44.0
Total		14	11	25	
Percent		56.0	44.0		100.0

Note: X^2 = 11.402. Significant at p = 0.001, with 1 df.

TABLE 3.6

Crosstabulation: Reputation by Families with no Employed Member

| | | Reputation Score | | Total | Percent |
		High	Low		
		100.0	9.1		
	Low				
		14	1	15	60.0
No workers					
			90.9		
	High				
			10	10	40.0
Total		14	11	25	
Percent		56.0	44.0		100.0

Note: X^2 = 14.973 with 1 df. Significant at p = 0.001.

TABLE 3.7

Crosstabulation: Reputation by Percent Apartments Vacated in 1969

| | | Reputation Score | | Total | Percent |
		High	Low		
		100.0	27.3		
	Low				
		14	3	17	68.0
Percent apartments vacant 1969					
			72.7		
	High				
			8	8	32.0
Total		14	11	25	
Percent		56.0	44.0		100.0

Note: X^2 = 14.973 with 1 df. Significant at p = 0.001.

differences in the variables making up the "child factor" group, the transiency group, and the phenomenon of community reputation.

SELECTION OF FOUR SUBJECT DEVELOPMENTS

With the above findings the problem of selecting several appropriately distinctive developments was made much easier. There were, however, several other factors to consider. First, since the study focused so closely upon the degree to which tenants are problems to managers, it was necessary to select developments where the managers were either of long tenure or, in the judgment of their superiors, were aggressive and alert enough to have become well acquainted with their tenant population. Second, although the correlations showed no significant relationship between racial composition and either reputation scores or specific management problems, the prevalence of community speculation regarding this variable compels its consideration.

With these criteria in mind the following developments were selected: Charlestown, Columbia Point, Mary Ellen McCormack (Old Harbor Village), and the South End (Cathedral) development. They represented a range of values along several of the most important parameters with which we are concerned, particularly on the reputation scale and in the child group variables. (See Table 3.8.)

It would have been possible to select developments representing higher transiency levels, but in all cases these also represent neighborhoods of rapid change of racial composition with all of the accompanying social tensions typical of such periods of transition. The experience of the BHA has shown that the turbulence of these periods is time-limited, in that once the incoming group is established as dominant in the entire area then both apartment turnover and incidents of racial conflict fall off markedly.* Because inclusion of such developments would introduce the effects of tensions based in the immediate intergroup problems existing in the surrounding neighborhood, Columbia Point was selected in preference to Bromley Park, which might have otherwise been included.

It would have been interesting to include in the sample one of those developments with a nonwhite population of 90 percent or more. However, these developments were either too small or their managers were too recently assigned to enable them to have become well acquainted with the tenant population. The South End, with over 60 percent black families (and a total population of 1,574) represents the highest black concentration in the sample.

Not only does this sample of four developments display a range of reputation scores, of racial composition, and of child group characteristics but it also offers a variety of architectural types, with high- and low-rise buildings and various mixtures of apartment sizes.

THE SAMPLE DEVELOPMENTS IN PROFILE

Briefly, then, let us examine the four target developments.

McCormack: This development is, of course, the most venerable. Constructed in the mid-thirties, its 1,018 units have been occupied since 1937. During that time it has been considered by staff and residents alike as one of the "best" projects. Although most of its structures are similar to the red-brick, three-story walkup apartments that were stereotypic of that period of public housing, it enjoys many pleasant architectural features that were later considered frills and eliminated from designs—balconies, larger penthouse apartments,

----

*The Orchard Park development went through such a cycle with black families replacing white families during the years 1962-67. After a transition period that was often tumultuous, social interaction in the development returned to a relative equilibrium once the racial ratio had stabilized.

TABLE 3.8

Target Developments by Selected Variables

Project	Number of Units	Reputation Score	Ratio: Child, to Males [a]	Percent Single-Parent Families	Percent 5 yrs. Occup.	Percent Nonwhite Families	Physical Structure
McCormack	1018	2.0 (high)	1:4.61	26	33	3	Low-rise
Charlestown	1146	3.3 (medium high)	1:4.03	35	33	1	Low-rise
South End	506	4.6 (low-medium)	1:6.31	45	39	61	Low- and high-rise
Columbia Pt.	1444	5.3 (low)	1:10.50	55	42	42[b]	Low- and high-rise

[a] Non-elderly adult males

[b] Because of high proportion of white elderly families, the actual nonwhite population for Columbia Point is 57 percent higher than the proportion of families would indicate.

extensive landscaping, and, in the management office, historical murals and wood carvings (mementoes of the spirit of the New Deal). From the outset, an apartment in Old Harbor Village was a coveted prize, and pressures upon the Authority for assignments there have been relentless through the years. This is reflected in its high score of two on the reputation scale and the fact that the speaker of the U.S. House of Representatives consented to have the development bear his mother's name.

The population, like that of the surrounding neighborhood, has always been predominantly white, Roman Catholic, and of Irish background. (The 3 percent black families are relatively recent arrivals.) Built primarily for young families with the assumption that this would be a temporary housing arrangement for most, the apartments are small—none with more than three bedrooms. Today a large proportion of the residents are older persons who have been assigned apartments there because of their limited space needs or who have grown old in residence. Fully 70 percent of the households have fewer than three members, and 57 percent of the heads of household are 60 years of age or older. Ten percent of the residents have lived there for over thirty years, 21 percent for over twenty years.

Partially because of the absence of large apartments and also because of the aging nature of its population, the McCormack project enjoys a ratio of children to non-elderly male adults of only 3.38 to 1, in contrast to some of the other developments where the ratio is greater than 10 to 1.

Over one-third of its households still obtain most of their income from employment, which is high for a public housing development in 1969. While 45 percent receive social security benefits, only 13 percent are on OAA and a mere 8 percent are on AFDC, lower than for the city as a whole (10 percent). This is remarkable in that 26 percent of the non-elderly families have only one parent, usually a woman. Many others would probably be eligible for aid if they would apply.

Charlestown: This development was constructed only shortly after McCormack, under the Housing Act of 1937. Though in scale (1,118 units) and design (three-story, red brick) it is quite similar to its older sister, it has never enjoyed the same high status in the neighborhood as that conferred upon McCormack, and its residents have had to contend with a certain stigma attached to them and their dwelling place by fellow Charlestowners. This is in spite of the fact that they share many of the same social characteristics with McCormack: all but 1 percent white and predominantly Irish Catholic (like the surrounding neighborhood), a relatively high proportion of employed tenants (38 percent), and a higher, but still relatively low, percentage dependent upon AFDC (16 percent). Charlestown has its share of

old-timers, with 13 percent having lived there for over 20 years;
and, again thanks in part to the high proportion of small apartments,
47 percent of its heads of household are over 60 years of age. There
are some very large apartments, but altogether only 13 percent of
the families have more than five members. Although the population
is somewhat younger, the ratio of non-elderly male adults to children
is still a low 1 to 4.03. The Reputation Score of the development,
in contrast to the other housing developments, is still a high-medium,
3.3.

South End: This development, known also as Cathedral Project,
is a product of the great building period of the early 1950s. Although
smaller in scale (506 units), it is a high-density development, the
tightly packed, elevator buildings of which present the viewer with a
monolithic if not monumental facade. Compactly designed, the project
resembles a step-pyramid with two-story buildings around the perim-
eter, banked against ascending tiers of higher buildings rising in
stages to a 14-story tower in the center of the block. Built of yellow
brick, the development stands in contrast to the red-brick storefronts
and bow-front town houses on the surrounding streets. Like the
McCormack and Charlestown developments it is adjacent to a large
Roman Catholic church (in this case, the Archdiocesan Cathedral),
although the population of this development has made less use of their
proximity than have tenants of the previously described projects.

The South End of Boston has always been a port of entry for
new minorities and is one of the most heterogeneous parts of the city.
The development reflects this, many of its older white tenants, including Greeks and Jews, representing the remnants of earlier immigra-
tion. More recent arrivals are reflected in the growing number of
black families (61 percent) and Puerto Ricans. The latter are as yet
unrecognized in the Tenant Status Review, having been counted in
both white and nonwhite categories depending on the interviewer's
judgment.

The South End Development has also been a residence greatly
sought after, but by a much more desperate group of applicants,
usually blacks or Puerto Ricans who have no housing but are eager
to live close to relatives and friends in the South End neighborhood.
The demand for these units has been further heightened by a great
deal of urban renewal activity in the area and widespread dislocation
of families. Characteristically, many of the relocated families were
economically dependent, single-parent, and nonwhite. Thirty-five
percent were on AFDC in 1969, and another 22 percent on OAA: 45
percent of the non-elderly families being single-parent, with a correspondingly higher ratio of children to adult, non-elderly males—
6.31 to 1.

In spite of the shifts occurring in the neighborhood around it, this development has not experienced a very high turnover: 39 percent have lived here only five years or less, but this is still below the mean for all housing developments and far below the 68 percent of the Heath Street development in Jamaica Plain.*

The distribution of ages of heads of household is much closer to the overall distribution in the public housing of Boston generally, with a characteristically high percentage of heads over 60 (36 percent), and a correspondingly large number of one- and two-person families (51 percent).

The South End development scored 4.6 on the Reputation Scale, about low-medium on the seven-point scale.

Columbia Point: Built in the puritanical style of the early 1950s, this is the largest development in New England (with 1,444 units available for occupancy) and the most highly visible development in Boston. Although its many elevator buildings are only seven stories high, their setting on a peninsula of land jutting out into Boston harbor exaggerates its profile to such an extent that most Bostonians refer to the buildings as though they were skyscrapers.

Columbia Point's very name has become an anti-public-housing scare word in the community, and its real or fancied evils are widely and successfully used by critics of the program. Thus, no public housing for families has been built in the city since Columbia Point opened its doors. Understandably, in view of the above, its reputation score is a low 5.3.

In spite of its negative public image and a chronic problem with vacancies, Columbia Point has enjoyed a relatively stable population, with only 42 percent of its families having moved in within the last five years. The rapid shift from white to black occupancy that was predicted in the mid-1960s has not come to pass, and, although 57 percent of the population is now black, it still accounts for a minority of the households (42 percent).

There is a stable group of largely white, elderly households occupying several buildings composed of smaller apartments near the far (ocean) end of the project. The majority of the remaining non-elderly households are black, 55 percent of which are also single-parent. Not surprisingly, the AFDC caseload in this development

----

*In that case the neighborhood had just experienced a rapid shift of racial composition, with whites moving out and being replaced by blacks. Experience in other parts of the city, namely the Orchard Park development, indicates that these situations are highly transitory and that within a few years the population will stabilize.

includes 41 percent of all families. Correspondingly, the number of families with any employed member falls to 25 percent.

It is in the child group variables identified in our analysis of variation among projects that Columbia Point differs drastically from the other target projects. Twenty-nine percent of the families at Columbia Point have more than five members, compared with only 8 percent in McCormack, and the ratio of adult non-elderly males to children is a high 1 to 10:50.

Here, then, are the four developments in which our study of problem tenants will be carried out. They are, as shown in the above review, representative of quite distinctive social and physical patterns. The following chapter will describe the methodology used during the field phase of the research.

NOTES

1. Richard Scobie, Social Analysis of the Tenant Population (Boston: Boston Housing Authority, 1970).
2. Alexander Ganz, Population and Income of the City of Boston (Boston: Boston Redevelopment Authority, Research Division Report, June, 1970).
3. Boston Area Study, Joint Center of Urban Studies, Harvard-Massachusetts Institute of Technology, 1970. Special runs completed at the request of the BHA.
4. Ibid.
5. Ibid.
6. Ibid.
7. Gerald Taube, A Family Album (Boston: Boston University, 1967).
8. L. S. Cronbach, "Test Reliability," Psychometrics, 1947, Number 12, pp. 1-16; and 1951, Number 16, pp. 294-334.

$$\text{Alpha} = \left(\frac{m}{m-1} \quad \frac{\sigma^2 \text{ total} - \Sigma\sigma^2}{\sigma^2 \text{ total}} \quad . \right)$$

9. David J. Armor, The Data-Text Primer: An Introduction to Computerized Social Data Analysis Using the Data-Text System (New York City: The Free Press, 1972).

4

METHODOLOGY AND FINDINGS

PRELIMINARY NEGOTIATIONS

Access to the Boston Housing Authority was no problem for the investigator, who had served as consultant to the administrator during the previous year and had already conducted the analysis of the Tenant Status Review (TSR) described earlier. With the verbal approval of the administrator to proceed with a pilot study, the investigator held a meeting with the director of management to secure his support and assistance. The director proved to be extremely helpful, understandably being interested in the practical implications of the work, and made it possible to move quickly into the field. The project selected for the test run was the D Street development in South Boston. It was chosen primarily because of the qualities of the manager, who was understanding, unthreatened, and articulate. It was his willingness to cooperate in this preliminary stage that enabled the investigator to test out and refine the methodology to be described below.

One particularly interesting finding in the dry run was that there were relatively few problem tenants identified in that part of the development that was notorious as a problem area. This suggested that the two phenomena, problem tenants and problem areas, might be more tenuously related than had always been supposed.

Later, a letter of endorsement was obtained from the acting administrator, along with a memorandum from the director of management to each of the four managers in the subject developments. This memo was the only correspondence the managers were to receive about the study, although all had had occasion to meet the investigator during the previous year. It outlined, briefly, the major steps that would be taken and the kind of assistance that was expected of the managers. Within the week of the distribution of the memo, calls were made to each manager for an initial appointment.

The field study portion of this research was divided into five distinct phases, which proceeded in series:
    phase 1—development of problem-tenant typology
    phase 2—identification of problem tenants and problem areas
    phase 3—the complaint log
    phase 4—gathering social and economic data
    phase 5—mapping.

PHASE 1: DEVELOPMENT OF A
PROBLEM-TENANT TYPOLOGY

Phase 1 of the field investigation consisted of interviews with each manager, during which he was asked to discuss his own views of the factors that lead him to consider a family to be a problem tenant. The purpose of this discussion was to develop from the manager's own testimony a typology of problem tenants that could be used in later phases. This technique was selected in preference to using an investigator-written typology that would prematurely lock in attitudes or lead the managers toward an emphasis on one type of behavior rather than another. Categories were solicited from each manager for inclusion in the typology, and after a draft typology was assembled copies were sent to each for his review, comment, or amendment. Few alterations or additions were offered; the final typology was essentially identical to the draft. The list of specific types of problems was grouped into broader categories both for ease of use in the field and to simplify coding procedures in later stages.
    Following is the problem-tenant typology:

General: Any tenant whose activity is detrimental to the welfare or peace of mind of other neighbors or management to such a degree that he becomes a problem tenant in the judgment of the management.

    A. Rule breaking and property damage
        1. Animals (uncontrolled)
        2. Chronic failure to clean halls when responsible
        3. Unauthorized tenant
    B. Administrative—chronic rent arrears.
    C. Health-related
        1. Senility or feebleness as special health condition requiring special protection or services
        2. Mental illness or retardation causing person to become a problem to management
        3. Alcoholism and alcohol-related disturbances
        4. Child neglect

D. Criminal or potentially antisocial activity (of any identified member of family)
   1. Theft via breaking and entering or handbag snatching
   2. Physical assault
   3. Sexual offenses
   4. Gang activity, such as intimidation or extortion
   5. Narcotics violations
   6. Child abuse or contributing to the delinquency of a minor
   7. Vandalism
E. Interpersonal problems (chronic)
   1. Verbal harrassment of neighbors, passersby, and staff
   2. Conflict over care of public areas, halls, and so on
   3. Conflict over child control or child rearing
   4. Other types of interpersonal conflicts (including persons being harrassed)
   5. Racial or ethnic conflict
   6. Chronic complaining
F. Sanitation-related practices
   1. Housekeeping problems severe enough to concern neighbors or management
   2. Sloppy disposal of refuse
G. Nuisance behavior
   1. Loud, disruptive noises, including parties, music, machines, and domestic quarrels
   2. Uncontrolled or disturbing child activity (more aggressive than E.3)
H. Multi-problem families—when several of the above categories are combined in one continuously and severely disruptive family.

It should be noted that the managers did not contribute evenly to the above typology (see Appendix D), and the emphasis that they placed in their descriptions of problem tenants in general was in some cases reflected in the kinds of specific problems they cited later in Phase 2. On the other hand, some of the problem types stressed during the initial interviews did not appear at all when managers were asked for specific cases.

PHASE 2: IDENTIFICATION OF PROBLEM TENANTS

Following the development of the problem-tenant typology a review was conducted with each manager of the entire tenant case-load in order to identify by name and apartment number families that the manager considered to be problems to him as manager—or problem tenants. At each step in the field study phases it was necessary to make the distinction between the problem tenant as a unit of study defined in terms of its having been identified as a problem by management and the problem family of more general fame. Several times managers had to be reminded that the investigator was not really interested in Mrs. A because she had problems but was interested only if Mrs. A presented a problem to the manager.

Classification of problem tenants according to the major presenting problem was done in discussion with the manager and based primarily upon his judgment. When a secondary problem was present it was noted. Families designated as multi-problem families were tenants representing three or more problem types. In each of these cases the level of disruption was so high that the appropriateness of the label was immediately accepted by both manager and investigator. This operational definition is consistent with that used by both Geismar and Pavenstedt, whose works were discussed in Chapter 2, with the exception that, unlike the Geismar study, we have no data that would substantiate intrafamily malfunction.

In order to reduce the effect that fatigue or boredom might have on the manager's judgment, we divided the task in half and completed in two morning interviews lasting about three hours each, except for the smaller South End development where one session was sufficient.

A total of 196 problem tenants were identified, with the manager in each case describing the situation or events that led to his or her judgment. Unfortunately, it was impossible to determine with any precision the amount of time that had elapsed between a problem episode and the interview, except when the problem was of quite recent origin. This was to cause some difficulty in the analysis phase.

At the end of each interview, each manager was given a site map of the development and asked to mark on it those sections that he considered to be, or which were generally known to be, problem areas. He was also asked to explain what he meant by a problem area and to try to give some reasons for the cited areas being identified as such.

Although the managers at first greeted the investigation with unequal enthusiasm, as the work progressed each appeared to give his complete support to the effort and to respond thoroughly and honestly to questions and requests at each stage of the research.

PHASE 3: THE COMPLAINT LOG

Phase 3 involved the keeping of a complaint log on which was recorded every instance of a complaint by or against a tenant family, the data of the complaint, the nature of the problem involved, and the action taken by the manager. The managers were told both verbally and in writing:

> Record every instance of a complaint about the activities of any member of a tenant family, whether it comes from another family, a member of the staff, or a community organization or agency. If this complaint comes from an anonymous source, record it. If you know the person registering the complaint but he asks to be kept anonymous, record his name and/or apartment number anyway. (This information will be used for statistical analysis only and names will be kept confidential.) The investigator will check with you frequently to see how the log is functioning and to answer any questions.

Managers were supplied with printed log forms and clipboards with pens attached. During the ten weeks in which the log was kept (from May 24 to July 30, 1971) they were interviewed at least once a week in person and telephoned in between interviews to monitor progress and answer questions about the recording of complaint incidents. During the ten-week period, a total of 61 entries were made involving 107 different families as complainers or complainees, either in combinations where both were known or when one or the other remained anonymous. Note was made when the same combination of complainer and complainee appeared repeatedly, but repeated identical entries were not made in the log. For this reason a greater number of new entries occurred during the first two weeks than in subsequent weeks.

PHASE 4: GATHERING SOCIAL
AND ECONOMIC DATA

With the identification of the managers' problem tenants and the families listed in the log, it was next necessary to gather a reliable body of data about each family. To do this the investigator turned to the case folders on each tenant kept in the local development office. In most instances, this information was drawn from the 1971 TSR form, although on some occasions the best data available had to be gleaned from a combination of application forms, pieces of correspondence, or TSR forms from previous years.

The 1971 TSR provided some information that had not been available before: the marital status of the head of household, the educational attainment, a more detailed breakdown of the racial and ethnic characteristics, and a notation of the primary language. Where the information was in "nominal type" categories, a coding system was devised to enable one to enter this information on IBM cards for computer manipulation. The problems cited by managers or, in the complaint log, by other tenants, were also reduced to code for analysis purposes. Finally, as cases were spotted on site maps for each development, such architectural or design features as whether or not an apartment was on a first floor, faced a street, or a court-yard, or was in an elevator building, and the mix of apartment sizes were also added to the coded information for each family.

PHASE 5: MAPPING

In order to determine the importance of architectural or eco-logical features in the identification of problem families or in the interaction of complaining and complained-about families site maps were secured for each of the four subject developments. These were products of different architectural firms and different times, drawn to different scales, and with design coding that was not always con-sistent. These maps were prepared for the spotting of problem cases in order to distinguish the buildings by the mix of apartment sizes contained in the structures, the presence of elevators, and the location of problem areas defined by the managers.

The mix of apartment sizes in each building was complicated to some degree because of the variety of combinations found in many developments. Six mutually exclusive types were defined:

1. Predominantly small apartments (1 or 2 bedrooms = 75 percent or more).
2. Small and medium-size apartments (1 and 3, or 2 and 3 bedroom structures in which 1 or 2 bedrooms = 50 percent or more).
3. Medium-size apartments (3, or 2 and 3 bedroom, or 3 and 4 bed-room apartments, where 4 bedrooms = less than 50 percent).
4. Large and medium-size apartments (5 and 3, or 4 and 3, where 4 or 5 bedroom apartments = 50 percent or more).
5. Large apartments (4 or 5 bedroom apartments = 75 percent or more).
6. Large and small apartments, mixed (1 or 2 and 4 or 5 bedroom apartments).

In most developments, it was possible to determine these cate-gories by examining the key of the official site maps, but at McCor-mack the coding proved to be so inaccurate that a building-by-building survey of sizes became necessary. High-rise buildings and problem areas identified by managers were noted and the maps then used to

locate management's problem tenants and to spot incidents of intertenant friction as indicated in the complaint log.

DATA HANDLING

A detailed description of the actual procedures undertaken in
the analysis appears in the appendix. Briefly, after families were
identified in the field as management problems or as entries on the
complaint log information on multiple social and economic variables
was extracted from the Housing Authority's records. This data was
then coded for ease of analysis, transferred to punched cards, and
analyzed quantitatively.

In all, we were handling information that addressed the scope
of the problem-tenant phenomenon in four diverse developments;
the types of problems encountered; the relationship of problem tenants to problem areas; the social characteristics of problem tenants;
the relationship of those characteristics to the aggressivity of the
problem; the variation among developments; the association of intertenant conflict with problem-tenant identification; and the importance
of social differences in that conflict.

FINDINGS*

The problem tenant was found to be a rather limited phenomenon,
making up from 2.2 percent (McCormack) to 4.1 percent (Columbia
Point) of the total tenant population. The average for the four developments when grouped was 3.4 percent. Families considered to be
multi-problem families represent only 15.6 percent of problem tenants for all developments, with a high of 28 percent at Columbia
Point where the largest proportion of families so identified were
found. The rest of the problem tenants represented other types of
problems, ranging from health problems to interpersonal difficulties
and antisocial behavior that, although serious, did not seem to be
part of the traditional multi-problem family constellation of woes.

There was considerable variation among the four target projects in the way problem tenants were distributed among general
problem categories. The proportion of severely disruptive problems
increased as the reputation of the projects fell, constituting only
4.5 percent at McCormack, 16.6 percent at Charlestown, 33.3 percent
at South End, and 49 percent at Columbia Point. The interpersonal

---

*For detailed findings see Appendix E.

types of problems distribute themselves in reverse order, with 77.2 percent at McCormack (made up mainly of verbal harrassment, chronic complaining, and child-control conflicts), 71.2 percent at Charlestown (with more emphasis on racial conflict), 26.6 percent at South End, and 26.4 percent at Columbia Point. Health problems do not vary greatly from project to project in the proportion of problems they represent, except at South End, where they peak at 40 percent. Rule breaking problems seem more related to management style than reputation, peaking in the projects with mid-range reputations (45.5 percent at Charlestown and 48.3 percent at South End) when all problem tenants, including the rule breakers, are considered together.

Problem areas in the developments did not seem to be clearly related to the presence of problem tenants or of instances of inter-tenant conflict. Of the 21 problem areas identified, clusters of three or more problem tenants occurred in only 11. Complaint-log cases occurred in only 11 of the 21 areas (not the same 11).

Social Characteristics of Problem Tenants

When the problem-tenant group itself is examined in terms of social and physical variables, only instances where the proportions differ widely from those found in the population as a whole are worthy of reemphasis here.

In regard to race, nonwhites did not represent a different proportion among the problem tenants than they did in any of the target developments as a whole, and only when crossed with problem type was it apparent that nonwhites were more often involved in severely disruptive problems, while whites accounted for most of the health problems. This pattern was most striking at Columbia Point, where severe cases involved antisocial or illegal activities rather than the anticipated multi-problem families.

When age of household head was examined, it was found that tenants over 60 years of age consistently represented only about one-quarter of the problem tenants, far less than their proportion in the population. As expected, both young and middle-aged families dominate both the rule breaking and severe disruption categories, while the elderly account for the health problems.

Female-headed households make up a larger proportion of problem tenants than they do in the overall population of all developments. They do not seem particularly disposed toward one type of problem or another.

Very large families present few health problems, and, unexpectedly, don't constitute a disproportionate share of the severe disruption cases either. Most of their difficulties fall into the interpersonal problems category.

Regarding tenure, there is a disproportionately large number of tenants with fewer than five years in occupancy across all categories of problem tenants everywhere except at McCormack, where older tenants appear with greater regularity.

Architectural variables were largely unassociated with problem-tenant distribution. Only inner-court entrances seemed to present a larger-than-expected proportion of problems, and then only in the low-rise developments.

When correlations were obtained for social variables with the problem type reordered in terms of aggressivity, only a few relationships were significant: race (with a positive correlation); age (with a negative correlation): family size (positive only at Charlestown and Columbia Point); and reputation of the development (negative). There was a slight negative correlation with years in occupancy and no correlation at all with sex of head of family or with the presence of employed members.

The Variation Among Developments

There was considerable variation among the four developments both in terms of volume of problem tenants and the types of problems expressed. This range appears to be related to the reputation phenomenon used in selecting the sample, with both number and severity of problems rising as the reputation falls. The social characteristics of problem tenants did not fall into any pattern or profile that was consistent across all four developments.

The Association of Intertenant Conflict with Problem-Tenant Identification

The complaint log, kept for ten weeks, yielded 61 entries, representing 117 families, of which 100 appeared in 50 interacting pairs of complainer and complainee. The complaints of the tenants about their neighbors were largely centered around interpersonal problems (57 percent) or severe disruption (33 percent) with little variation in these proportions between developments.

There was an overlap between managers' problem tenants and complaint log appearances of 23 cases, making up 17.3 percent of the problem tenants already identified. Seven of these were complainers; 14 were complainees. While there was some difference between the problems perceived by managers and tenants in this overlapping group these differences were not serious, and there was no evidence that managers were being more negative in their judgments than were the tenants.

Conflict among tenants as expressed in entries on the complaint logs proved to be highly related to the identification of families as problem tenants in all developments except South End. In three out of four developments, the ratio of problem tenants among complaint-log entries to all entries differed positively from the ratio of all problem tenants to the total population at a very high level of significance.

The Importance of Social Differences
in Intertenant Conflict

When the roles tenants play in the interaction (complainer or complainee) were crossed by social and architectural variables the findings were generally negative, with a few exceptions. At Columbia Point there was some evidence that while whites frequently complained about nonwhites the few nonwhites making complaints only complained against other nonwhites. When the four projects were grouped, the amount of education was found to be related with complaint log role, those with less than a high-school education appearing with greater regularity among the complainers; but this did not hold for individual developments. Architecturally, the only factor that appeared related to complaint-log role was first-floor occupancy, with most of those being complained about occupying first-floor apartments.

In general, it was found that incidents of intertenant conflict in these four developments took place more often between similar families than between dissimilar families. Conclusions drawn from these findings will be discussed in relation to the original hypotheses and research questions, along with their implications for management, social science theory, and public policy in the following and final chapter.

CHAPTER

5

CONCLUSIONS AND IMPLICATIONS

CONCLUSIONS

In Chapter 2 several hypotheses and research questions were posed. First we asked just how many tenants there are whom management considers to be problems; what types of problems they represent; how they are different from their neighbors, either socially or by their location in the project; and how the picture differs from development to development. Next we asked whether intertenant conflict might be related to the labeling of certain families as problem tenants; and, having established that, we asked whether social or architectural differences were associated with the roles tenants played in that conflict.

All of this was done in order to have a clear picture of just who problem tenants are, what makes them problems, and whether there is anything special about them. It was also posited that tenant conflict, perhaps based on social differences, might be a better explanation of who gets labeled than are the traditional pathological models.

When those families whose identification as problem tenants was due to administrative rule breaking were omitted, it was found that a very small proportion of the tenants in any of the four developments were labeled as problem tenants by management. This proportion ranged from a low of 2.2 percent at McCormack (the highest reputation development) to 4.1 percent at Columbia Point (the lowest reputation development).

The group classified as multi-problem families represented only 15.6 percent of the problem cases, overall, and a little over one-quarter of the problems at Columbia Point—still a tiny proportion of the entire tenant body. While a few cases were identified because of health-related difficulties and a larger number involved problems classified as severely disruptive, most problem tenants fell into the interpersonal problems categories. Even among those classified as severely disruptive there was a clear absence of what might be called assaultive behavior.

The problem tenants themselves differed from their neighbors along some social variables, but not others. The elderly lived up to their reputation as ideal tenants by making up a smaller proportion of the problem-tenant group than their number in the entire population would have predicted. Female-headed households appeared with greater frequency among the problem tenants than in the population as a whole. Nonwhite families appeared among the problem tenants in almost the expected proportion, but race did seem to be related to the type of problem being expressed, nonwhites appearing more frequently among those cases identified as severely disruptive than their numbers might have predicted. Family size, composition, length of occupancy, and economic dependence were not significantly associated with the labeling of a family as a problem tenant.

If one were asked to sketch the profile of a typical problem-tenant family on the basis of this data, one might with some degree of certainty describe it as non-elderly. With considerably less confidence, one might add that the family would probably be female-headed. Little more could be said with certainty. The typical problem would be one fitting the interpersonal category, although this might vary with the reputation of the development, with a greater likelihood that the problem would be more severe in low-reputation projects. That the family would be identified as a multi-problem family would be unlikely, especially in the high-reputation developments.

The only architectural feature that seemed at all related to the distribution of problem tenants was the inner-courtyard entrance but only in the low-rise developments. Other features that have been the subject of much speculation over the years—high-rise buildings, the mix of apartments, and the concentration of large apartments— all appeared to be unrelated to the presence of problem tenants. These factors did, however, appear to be related somewhat to those areas in the developments described by managers as problem areas, this being particularly so of high concentrations of large apartments and a corresponding large number of children. Overall, there was little relationship between the presence of families designated by managers as problem tenants and areas designated by the same managers as problem areas.

The developments differed from each other both in the number of problems identified and in the proportion of those problems that fell into the severely disruptive group. Thus, with the number of severely disruptive cases rising as the reputation of the development fell, the earlier supposition that the reputation would be closely associated with the number and type of problems found was strengthened.

By comparing the proportion of previously identified problem tenants appearing on the complaint logs with the proportion of all problem tenants appearing among the entire population of each development, we found a highly significant difference. In three out of four developments a family's appearance on the complaint log was strongly associated with their being considered a problem tenant.

There were few significant associations of the social characteristics of the interacting tenants and the roles they played on the complaint logs. It must therefore be concluded that social differences, at least those examined in this study, do not play a major part in intertenant conflicts.

Some variables appeared to be associated with role on the complaint logs at single developments but failed to emerge as significant across the entire sample. Among these were sex of the head of the household (a significant factor only at Charlestown where female-headed households represented a disproportionate share of the families complained about), and race (which appeared to be significant only at Columbia Point where whites complained about a disproportionate number of blacks while blacks, when they complained at all, did so against other blacks). Education appeared to be related to role but only when all four developments were grouped; this, however, did not hold for individual developments.

Other variables, many of which figure prominantly in the literature, proved insignificant when examined in terms of their distribution between roles on the complaint logs. Among these were age, the source of income (dependency), family size, age of children, and years in occupancy.

Of all the architectural factors examined, only first-floor occupancy appeared to be associated with the role played by tenants in complaint incidents. It was earlier speculated that additional stress, in the form of all the noise and litter that is likely to characterize an entryway, might make first-floor occupancy a factor in intertenant conflict. To some extent this was confirmed, with first-floor families more frequently the target of complaints.

Thus, in summary, the hypothesis that intertenant conflict is rooted in social dissimilarities that, in turn, are influenced by architectural design was not borne out in this study, with the few exceptions already noted.

IMPLICATIONS

The very thoroughness with which the "social differences= conflict" hypothesis has been rejected compels a reassessment of many of the ideas on which it was based and a discussion of the implications all of these findings may have for the practice of housing management, for social science theory, and for social policy as it affects the housing field.

Implications for Housing Management

There are four major implications for housing management that will be discussed here: the need for a reassessment of both the magnitude of the problem-tenant problem and the types of difficulties that cause most tenants to be so defined; the importance of project reputation and the process of recall in influencing the perceptions of managers; the role of social services in the face of these findings; and some management strategies for handling the problem tenant.

First, in several ways it was shown that the perceptions of housing-management professionals through the years of the nature of the problem may have differed markedly from reality. Not only did the entire group of identified problem tenants represent a much smaller proportion of the total population of all developments than the literature might have led us to expect but the proportion of that group made up of families meeting criteria as multi-problem families was far smaller than might have been anticipated. There were certainly a few families that did meet the criteria for this label and surely they were extremely troublesome to management, but in numbers they simply did not justify the popular vision of housing developments filled with multi-problem families. Even at Columbia Point, where there were most families so identified, they represented only a tiny percentage of the entire population.

Although the proportion of problem tenants in no case rose above five percent of the tenant body, the variation among developments indicates a relationship between the reputation of a development and either the population mix, the kind of tenants, or the aggressivity of the problems being encountered. It is impossible, of course, to determine from this data which way the relationship goes. Nevertheless, managers of high-reputation developments (likely to have a large proportion of relatively problem-free elderly tenants) will need to spend roughly one-half of their time handling problem tenants, as will their colleagues in the low-reputation developments. This indicates that in assigning management personnel to low-reputation developments housing authorities should strive to select persons with the ability to be fair minded and flexible in dealing with human relationships. They should be sensitive to the kinds of social and health problems that require professional help, but in dealing with the immediate problems of management they need to be comfortable in the use of direct, short-term intervention rather than in reliance upon long-term treatment solutions with resultant stresses due to scarcity of resources.

Within developments the assumed association of problem areas with problem tenants will also have to be reassessed. Except for incidents of aggressive vandalism where a particular family or building appears to have been a target, the presence of problem tenants does not seem to have had a direct bearing on whether or not a space within a development would become a problem area. Rather, it has seemed to be issues of child density (to be treated further, below) and uses of the space in question in ways that may not have been anticipated by the architect.

Second, it is clear that there are factors affecting management perceptions that go beyond the immediate behavior of tenants, either singly or in interaction with one another. This is apparent from the areas of discrepancy between the problem-tenant typology and those problem types actually identified and the fact that the overlap between the group of manager-identified problem tenants and those appearing on the complaint log was not even greater than it was. Many families identified as problem tenants were noticeably absent during the ten weeks the log was kept.

There are two factors that may be playing an important role in the process through which a manager perceives his problems and attributes them to specific tenants. One of these is the length and intensity of recall; the other is the importance of a project's reputation in the perceptions of both tenants and staff.

It was impossible, during the data collection, to determine the passage of time between the events that had originally brought a given family to the attention of a manager and the interview, at which time the manager was being asked to make a judgment regarding a family's status as a problem tenant. Thus, it is also impossible to estimate the extent to which the list of problem tenants represents tenants who are currently involved in difficulties and to what extent it is made up of tenants who presented a problem some time in the past that is still fresh in the manager's mind. Managers may, having been impressed with the circumstances around a given complaint, amplify and exaggerate it into a "star" case, which retains its problematic aura long after the manifest problems have been resolved. This may be particularly true when the incident involves highly disruptive or aggressive behavior.

It would be important in any further attempts to define the problem tenant with greater accuracy to determine the length of time a family may continue to be considered a problem after the incident that first brought them to the manager's attention. It might further be of value to determine the additional length of time that a type of problem is retained in the mind of the manager as a relevant problem category even though the association with a specific family has been forgotten. It is in relation to the latter suggestion that the recollection of discrete occurrences may begin to merge with the effect of the reputation of a development upon the persons living and working there.

In a development that already has a poor reputation a manager may be influenced by the expectation of having many problem families to retain his judgment about a given family long after the precipitating event that caused that family to be noticed. When both tenants and staff have common expectations based on the low reputation of a development, this fact alone may further reinforce negative judgments once they have been made in a specific case. Thus a tenant occupying an apartment in a low-reputation development may, indeed, be quicker to apply problem family labels to the neighbors than he would be were he residing in a high-reputation project; and once a family has been singled out by neighbors or staff the manager may be more likely to accept the label and treat the family accordingly. Similarly, staff members who expect to find certain types of families in a given development will be likely to pass on to the manager information that is consistent with this expectation.

A similar mechanism may also operate within a development to help maintain the designation of certain areas as problem areas once they have been so labeled. That responses to situations that become habitual can remain institutionalized long after the original situation has changed is well known, and it is not improbable that similar mechanisms may be at work here. It may be that the notoriety of an area within a development lives on long after the initial incidents have been forgotten and that this reputation is reinforced by the mutual expectations and assumptions about the area held by both tenants and staff. William Whyte's finding in Park Forest that certain yards continued to produce the same patterns of activity long after the original residents had moved out would be consistent with these speculations.[1]

The reputation of a development may, then, through the circular and reinforcing process of labeling problem tenants that occurs in part as a result of that reputation, be a key factor in the career of an entire development. While the data collected here does not specifically support or refute this possibility, the discrepancies noted between typology and problems actually cited and the absence of many cited problem tenants from the complaint logs suggest that something beyond immediate occurrences is influencing the perceptions of management, both at the project level and in the total system.

Third, the role of social services as they exist as an adjunct to or as an integral part of housing management may also have to be

67

reexamined. Since the earliest days of public housing a debate, as described in Chapter 1, has raged over the appropriate role of social services in housing management. The question has not been, however, whether social services could be helpful in dealing with problem tenants but rather whether or not such services should be the direct responsibility of housing management. The character of the services themselves and the spirit with which they were offered has been largely dependent upon the conviction dominant in any given community about the nature of the housing agency itself.

Public housing can be viewed in at least two ways: as a public charity designed and operated as a minimum, stop-gap program for those in need; or, more generously, as one tool in a broader system of housing subsidies available as a public utility for all citizens. Within the context of the first conception social services might function as a kind of peacekeeping activity designed primarily to eliminate or head off problems that might interfere with or complicate the traditional tasks of property management. On the other hand, if the second conception is dominant social services might be seen as an important amenity available to residents as part of a wide system of services and programs designed to create a richer and more supportive social environment.

If the dominant conception of the nature of the housing program is the former—and this has been most common—then social services may be of limited value. Most of the problems cited that brought problem tenants to the attention of managers were not of the kind that might have been predicted or prevented by social service interventions; and, while social services might be helpful in assisting a very few families in weathering a crisis, it is known that they will have only limited impact when the difficulties are combined in a genuine multi-problem family.[2] Social services that are employed with the expressed intention of reducing management headaches over problem tenants will probably be a disappointment.

If, however, the dominant concept of the nature of the housing program is the latter, social services take on a broader meaning. In this case they stand on their own as a valuable benefit to the residents of a development. Unable to guarantee that the manager will have fewer problem tenants, they will instead offer a variety of services that become an integral part of any "suitable living environment" in the most positive sense of that famous phrase. Dealing with the intrafamilial problems of a young family under the stress of illness, finding employment or day care resources for a young mother, or helping to establish a recreation program for the elderly will probably not reduce the number of tenants that a manager ultimately will consider to be problems. Their value and justification must lie elsewhere, in the conviction that a good housing development means more than simply the absence of problems.

Fourth, the findings of this study have some implications for the strategies available to managers who must deal with those tenants they have determined to be problems. While unable to demonstrate that the social differences examined here played an important role in causing intertenant conflict, we did establish that conflict between tenants was itself highly associated with the identification of problem tenants. Intertenant conflict deserves the serious attention of management.

A direct way of dealing with intertenant conflicts, short of eviction, might be a more generous use of intradevelopment transfers. This strategy has been used frequently in the past with considerable success, particularly at Columbia Point. The number of vacancies and the rate of turnover will, of course, affect the extent to which this technique can be used, for there are invariably demands for apartments from new applicants with priority needs. However, there should be some administrative provision to insure that a reasonable proportion of vacancies are made available to the manager to deal with problems of intertenant conflict.

Another approach, already in wide use and to be encouraged, is the mediation of disputes by the manager or by selected members of his or her staff. Since intertenant conflict does not appear to be based on gross social differences, it may be more responsive to intervention by a respected manager. In these cases, as in most others, the paramount quality required of the manager is a sensitivity to the humanity of both parties and the ability to be flexible. Once a complaining tenant has had what he feels is a fair hearing, or once he has been offered a transfer (which he, in fact, may not even accept) many potential problem tenants will simply not be heard from again.

Implications for Social Science Theory

In this section we shall discuss three areas in which the findings contain implications for social science theory: intertenant conflict as a product of either heterogeneous or homogeneous social groupings; the continuing debate over the individual or interactional determinants of intertenant conflict; and, the impact of physical design upon social behavior, specifically upon interactions resulting in conflict.

First, the findings of this study shed some light on the effects that heterogeneity and homogeneity may have upon the quality of interaction taking place in a social setting such as a housing development. Interaction between neighbors has been generally sought as a social good by architects and housing administrators who ventured opinions on their own social objectives.[3] The suspicion on the part of these professionals was that interaction between neighbors would be intensified when those neighbors were socially similar; this hypothesis was further strengthened by Rosow's studies of housing of the elderly.[4] It was the related but not contrary possibility that the interaction between socially dissimilar neighbors might frequently result in conflict, as suggested by Gans' work in Levittown[5] that led us to the hypothesis that conflict based on social dissimilarities might be a major factor in the identification of problem tenants. This hypothesis was not supported by the findings.

We posited a model in which socially similar families would be expected to react positively with one another while socially dissimilar families would be expected to react negatively with one another. This was a reasonable model in view of the Gans observations and of other studies establishing a link between negative attitudes and social dissimilarities.[6] The failure of the data to support this model suggests an alternative in which socially similar families may interact in ways that are either harmonious or conflict laden, while dissimilar families may simply fail to interact. This second model is supported by the finding that the families interacting on the complaint logs in this study were far more likely to be similar than dissimilar in terms of the social variables being examined.

The only variable that might tend to support the original hypothesis (similar families interact harmoniously; dissimilar families interact unharmoniously) and challenge our alternative model (similar families interact; dissimilar families fail to interact) is that of education. The reader may recollect that a disproportionate share of non-high-school graduates appeared among the complainers in the complaint exchanges in the four grouped developments. Such a general result might have been anticipated in view of Taube's findings. In his sample there was a good deal of antagonism expressed by young, intact, employed white families toward their living environment and their neighbors when they were residing in developments characterized by high transiency and a prevalence of black, female-headed families.[7] Yet at Columbia Point, where this is the case, we found a less significant association between education and complaint log role than had been present when all four developments were grouped.

Furthermore, when the complaint instances at Columbia Point are examined in more detail it becomes clear that if the hostile attitudes reported by Taube exist they are not converted into active complaints with any regularity. Of all whites (both high-school graduates and nongraduates) only one family was intact and employed. The rest were all female-headed units. This would seem to indicate that although hostile attitudes may exist between dissimilar neighbors they are not likely to express themselves actively in the form of complaints by one against the other. This would be consistent with the second model, suggesting once again that dissimilar families are

unlikely to interact at all and, having failed to interact, they will therefore not come into open conflict. Thus a highly heterogeneous neighborhood might be expected to produce a low level of interaction and,
therefore, fewer reported conflicts that would come to the attention
of a housing manager.

Second, it would appear at first glance that the individual
pathology explanation of problem-tenanthood has not been seriously
challenged by the interactional theory as formulated in this study.
While conflict between tenants was shown to be closely associated
with the identification of problem tenants, certainly the gross social
differences examined here failed to be associated significantly with
the roles tenants played in the process of registering those complaints.
On the other hand, there was no evidence that the conflicts, except
for a few in which mental illness or alcoholism played a part, were
based upon pathological difficulties in one or both of the participants.
Certainly the scarcity of multi-problem families among those identified
as problem tenants puts in question the importance of that particular
brand of pathology. Since fewer multi-problem families become
problem tenants than do not and since many families who are not
multi-problem families nevertheless become problem tenants, other
factors must be at work here.

An interactional explanation may yet provide a more adequate
framework within which to approach the problem of the problem
tenant, but clearly the similarities and dissimilarities examined will
have to be far less obvious than those used in the current study. For
instance, it is possible that the otherwise similar families observed
to be in conflict on the complaint logs may differ in other important
respects, specifically in the adaptive mechanisms they have acquired
in their past experience. These may be akin to differences of social
class or considerations of life style referred to in Chapter 2. Explo-
ration of this possibility would require much more refined information
than was available to this investigator but might in the long run prove
to be more fruitful than a full retreat to explanations which continue
to stress individual pathology.

Third, the findings have some limited implications for archi-
tecture and the design of housing developments. The question of the
importance of architectural features to problem-tenanthood was
introduced as a correlate to the major hypothesis that emphasized
difference-based conflict. If the social differences under study
were truly important in bringing about conflict between tenants, then
the architectural features that determined the kinds of families that
might be housed together (particularly as they differ in size and age)
would be worthy of analysis. With the prior finding that most of the
social differences themselves are not significant factors in the
identification of problem tenants, much of the concern over the design
of the building becomes inconsequential.

Only in respect to the first-floor apartments is there any finding that might be related to writings that have concentrated on the social impact of physical design. It was Festinger[8] who first stressed the importance of strategic locations that increase the likelihood of chance meetings to subsequent forms of interaction. Families occupying first-floor, entryway apartments and those adjacent to stairways tended, in Festinger's study, to relate more frequently and in larger numbers to their neighbors than to families occupying apartments on upper floors or in the middle of hallways. In the current study it was, therefore, speculated that first-floor apartments might be a focus of negative interaction between neighbors as well, and this did materalize on the complaint log.

Inner courtyard designs, which were also considered by Festinger, Whyte, and others[9] to be conducive to positive types of neighborly interaction were examined to see if they might not be similarly conducive to negative interaction. There was some evidence that this might be the case in the two low-rise developments, McCormack and Charlestown, where a disproportionate share of the problem families resided in courtyard addresses; but at South End the courtyard addresses were no more frequently the homes of problem tenants than other locations. Recently the cul-de-sac nature of many court designs and the difficulty of policing these areas have given rise to many safety-oriented criticisms of such arrangements.[10] However valid these comments may be, there is no substantial indication from this data that inner courtyards tend to amplify intertenant conflict.

Thus the theories that emphasize the importance of physical proximity in the development of interaction between families have been borne out by the increased levels of conflict found around first-floor apartments. The extent to which this principle can also be further confirmed by our experience with conflict in the public spaces affected by a courtyard entrance is questionable.

Finally, one architectural characteristic that has been the subject of considerable speculation is the effect of the juxtaposition of very large and very small apartments within single apartment buildings. Would this practice, by placing single and presumably elderly persons next to large families with many children, lead to conflict and, subsequently, to the identification of the parties to that conflict as problem families? As might be expected from the previous discussion of the nonimportance of age and size-of-family variables, the effect of this architectural arrangement was negligible. In all four developments with a total of 21 stairhalls around which 288 very large and very small apartments were mixed, only one complaint incident took place during the ten weeks during which the complaint logs were kept.

Implications for Social Policy

This study has implications for three important social policy questions: who should be housed; in what kind of buildings they should be housed; how those who are to be housed should be located within the structures that are to be built. We shall deal with these in reverse order, moving from the specific to the general.

First, the process of tenant selection and placement has long been considered the administrative cornerstone of a sound occupancy policy. The traditional gate-keeping roles played by tenant selection officers have already been discussed in Chapter 1. It has been shown that the values and social attitudes of tenant-selection staff can have a profound impact on the social structure of different housing developments. This fact is reflected, at least in part, in the great diversity of developments along racial lines and other social variables. It has also been suspected for some time that the tenant-selection process could be used just as effectively in the creation, within developments, of healthier and happier mixes of tenants. While this study does not probe the degree to which tenants are pleased with the social context in which they live, it does, by examining the reverse side of the coin (expressions of dissatisfaction in the form of specific complaints about neighbors), shed some light on the question of tenant mix. The light it sheds, however, will not be encouraging to those who have hoped for some systematic formula that could be used to guide decisions regarding the composition of a given apartment structure.

With conflict between tenants as our unit of measure, we found no strong indications that social differences between tenants are likely to stimulate conflict between them. There was no evidence that differences of age, size of family, sex of head of household, source of income, or age of children had any bearing whatever on frequency of occurrences of conflict between tenants. Tenant selection officers, then, if they are implementing a policy that is concerned with reducing tenant conflict, might be advised to simply assign tenants on a random basis. If conflicts do arise after some time in occupancy, the managers should, as discussed earlier, have considerable freedom to reassign them to other apartments within the same development.

Second, policy questions regarding design are also addressed in this study, but the negative findings regarding the importance of social mix considerably diminish the extent to which this question can be answered definitively. As noted above, tenant conflict may at times be focused in first-floor entryways, but it is difficult to conceive of architectural solutions to that problem. It might be possible to reduce the number of points in an apartment design at which the interaction of tenants is bound to be higher, but tenant conflict as examined in this study did not prove to be serious enough to merit a design solution that would simultaneously diminish the possibility of positive interaction as well.

It is around the question of problem areas within the development that the findings of the study relate more directly to questions of design. The problem tenant presents managers with one multifaceted class of problem. Problem areas in the development apparently present the manager with a problem of another class. Thus, while buildings that are designed to house large numbers of very large families may not, in fact, produce a disproportionate share of problem tenants or many instances of tenant conflict, they may, nevertheless, be contributing to the existence of problem areas. Design does this by creating large concentrations of large families with children, as at Columbia Point and Charlestown, or an unintended play-yard when other facilities are inadequate, as at McCormack, or an unplanned pedestrian "short-cut" as at Columbia Point. The latter two examples involve questions of public-area design that are not directly addressed here. The former, however, may merit some comment on the basis of the findings of this study.

The concentration of large apartments in single buildings seems to lead frequently to the development of problem areas for management simply because of the increased wear and tear on the physical plant. In some areas it is not uncommon for over one hundred children to be using a single front door and a single elevator, a condition that is bound to result in chronic maintenance problems. Since there is no evidence here that a mix of family sizes would lead to conflict (but, on the contrary, that it is like families that tend to interact negatively), it might be wiser to scatter the larger units throughout the development. If buildings were designed to insure that no more than one very large family could be housed on a floor the problem areas in developments that are clearly related to child density might be eliminated.

Third, and most important, is the question of who should be housed. As discussed in Chapter 1, housers have from the beginning sought a way of screening out, or of identifying for special placement, the problem tenant. They have done this by concentrating on the problem family—by describing, analyzing, excluding, or treating them. Finally, and more recently, the new pessimists have broadened problem-family definitions to include whole categories of dependent or lower-class families and called for their exclusion or isolation in special enclaves set apart from the presumably less problematic working poor. Such strategies are needed, according to some,[11] in order to save public housing from the flight of its stable population and eventual decline. Although these opinions fly in the face of evidence that the emptying out of urban areas is also occurring in private areas where housing abandonment has reached vast proportions (even in St. Louis, the home of the disastrous Pruitt-Igoe project),[12] they continue to gain in popularity.

The findings of this study should not be encouraging to either the housing hardliners who advocate stricter screening to eliminate problem tenants before they get in or the softliners who advocate rehabilitative programs to deal with problem tenants once they have been housed.

As for the possibility of screening, it does not appear that the problem tenants identified in this study can be reduced to any simple profile that might enable tenant-selection personnel to make wiser judgments. While there are certain variables that appear with greater frequency among the problem tenants than the proportion they represent in the population as a whole, in no case is the difference great enough to justify the exclusion of eligible applicants. It is certainly impossible to predict what the performance of an applicant will be when he has become a tenant on the basis of the kind of social data that is available to tenant-selection officers. To act as if such predictions were justifiable would not only be illegal in light of current court decisions but unsupportable by all that we have learned here about the identity of problem tenants and the nature of the problems they present.

The suggestions that there is a deep-seated irritation on the part of the working poor toward their economically dependent neighbors, particularly when they are headed by black females on AFDCs, were simply not evident in the findings of this study. While female-headed households were most often complained against at Charlestown, this pattern did not reappear at any of the other three developments, regardless of reputation. Whether a family received its income from employment or through some form of transfer payment or benefit program was not a relevant factor in the distribution of incidents of conflict between tenants.

The concluding implication, then, must be that this study of problem tenants and of the process through which they are identified gives no support to the arguments that by screening out problem families or dependent families, or any other general category, we might be able to produce relatively problem-free residential areas.

Certainly there are serious problems in housing that are obvious to any observer. Yet for too long we have used the pursuit of the problem family or the problem tenant as a mechanism for avoiding harder questions about the inadequacy of our entire system of producing and managing subsidized housing. This study suggests strongly that it may now be time to bury the old myths and to stop looking for ways to blame systemic problems on presumed individual pathology.

NOTES

1. William Whyte, The Organization Man (Garden City, N.J.: Doubleday and Co., 1957).

2. See L. Geismar and Beverly Ayres, Patterns of Change in Problem Families (St. Paul, Minnesota: Family Centered Project, 1959).

3. Elizabeth Wood, Housing Design; A Social Theory (New York: Citizens Housing and Planning Council, 1961); Christopher Alexander, "The City as a Mechanism for Sustaining Human Contact," in William Ewald, Jr., ed., Environment for Man (Bloomington: Indiana University Press, 1967); Catherine Bauer, "Social Questions in Housing and Community Planning" in Journal of Social Issues 7 nos. 1, 2 (1951).

4. Irving Rostow, Social Integration of the Aged (New York: The Free Press, 1967).

5. Herbert Gans, The Levittowners (New York: Random House, 1967).

6. Gerald Taube, "The Social Structural Sources of Residential Satisfaction and Dissatisfaction in Public Housing" (Ph.D. Dissertation, Brandeis University, Waltham, Massachusetts, 1972).

7. Ibid.

8. Leon Festinger, Stanley Schacter, and Kurt Bock, Social Pressure in Informal Groups: A Study of Human Factors in Housing (New York: Harper, 1950).

9. Whyte, op. cit.

10. Oscar Newman, "Physical Parameters of Defensible Space: Past Experience and Hypotheses" (article in mimeo, Columbia University, 1969).

11. Roger Starr, "Which of the Poor Shall Live in Public Housing," The Public Interest, Spring 1971; Edward Banfield, The Unheavenly City: The Nature and Future of Our Urban Crisis (Boston: Little, Brown and Co., 1968).

12. National Urban League, The National Survey of Housing Abandonment (New York: National Urban League, 1972), pp. 21-27.

Daniel Finn, Administrator (1969-71)

Julius Bernstein, Chairman

John Connolly, Member

Doris Bunte, Member

Elaine Werby, Chief Social Planner

John Plunkett, Public Information Officer

Lloyd Howard, Director of Tenant Selection

George Bailey, Manager, South End Development

Mary Thompson, Acting Manager, Columbia Point Development

John Kelly, Manager, Charlestown Development

Andrew Walsh, Manager, Mary Ellen McCormack Development

APPENDIX B:
DATA HANDLING AND
THE DATA CODE BOOK

DATA HANDLING

The information collected from the Tenant Status Review census materials at each development was recorded in the field into a data book. Interval data was recorded directly while nominal categories were recorded in code. To facilitate the transfer of the data to 80-column IBM cards a code book was constructed, the coded data was arranged by column on Fortran Coding Forms, and the cards subsequently punched. Data was divided into batches: Batch One representing the managers' problem tenants and Batch Two representing information from the complaint logs.

Data processing was undertaken on the IBM 360 computer at Harvard University and was completed on the IBM 370 at the Massachusetts Institute of Technology through the Harvard remote terminal. The Armor and Couch Data-Text System for computerized social data analysis was used throughout.[1] On the initial set of Batch One runs, frequencies were obtained for all variables as coded, with separate totals for the four target developments grouped and for the individual developments separately. Only on later runs were variables collapsed into dichotomous categories or reordered for ease and clarity of analysis. The first set of runs yielded a picture of the problem-tenant population as actually identified by the managers of the four developments, which will be described below.

The second set of Batch One runs involved more ambitious objectives than simple description; therefore, in preparation, the data had to be redefined in certain ways. First, for the purpose of limiting the number of cells appearing in crosstabulations, several variables were reduced to three-part, or, if possible, dichotomous categories. The most critical variable thus collapsed was that describing the type of problem associated with each problem tenant. The original coding had included eight categories: rule breaking; administrative problems including rent arrears; health-related problems including mental illness and alcoholism; antisocial and potentially criminal activity; interpersonal problems; sanitation-related problems; nuisance behavior; and multi-problem families. These were collapsed into four: rules; health; interpersonal; and severe disruption.

The creation of these general problem types involved some difficult decisions about the classification of certain specific problems. For instance, while "uncontrolled child activity" was always considered more aggressive than "conflict over child control," they were both placed in the interpersonal problems type rather than placing the former in with the severe disruption cases. This was done in order to distinguish this from truly assaultive child behavior, which would, as antisocial or potentially criminal in nature, have been placed in the severe disruption category. The vandalism cases that made their way onto the list were of such severity (for example, the "bombing-out" of an entire apartment and the destruction of an automobile) that this otherwise common problem designation was placed in the severe disruption category. "Contributing to the delinquency of a minor" involved, in each case, selling alcoholic beverages to minors; therefore this was not placed in the severe disruption type.

The second set of Batch One runs provided frequencies based on the newly created categories for use in comparison of problem tenants with the known population of each development and with tenants appearing later on the complaint log; and crosstabulations and tests of association between individual social, economic, or architectural variables with the type of problem expressed.

In addition to providing this basis for analysis of the association of variables with the problem type, the data were also redefined in ordinal terms to make it possible to test, through the calculation of correlation coefficients, the degree of association of all variables with all other variables. In this case, the variable describing the type of problem was redefined in terms of the "aggressivity" (the degree of aggressiveness) inherent in the type of problem cited.

It was soon apparent that the inclusion of the rules category in all levels of the analysis was unnecessary and, indeed, would be detrimental to the testing of the theoretical propositions posed in the study. Therefore, on the third set of Batch One runs the rule-breaking problems were omitted. Other than this change, the third set of runs duplicated the program and instructions used for the second set. Thus, frequencies, crosstabulations with tests of significance, and correlations were obtained for all management problem tenants and management problems excluding the administrative rule-breaking categories.

Batch Two, the data obtained from the four complaint logs, was arranged using the same variable definitions already employed for Batch One. However, because tenants appearing on the log did so in a variety of roles (as complainer, complainee, both, subject of an anonymous complaint, or accuser of an unknown party), the handling became somewhat more complicated. Since an appearance on the log in any of the above roles was considered an index of conflict between tenants, frequencies and crosstabulations of variables with the type of problem as expressed by the complaining tenant were first obtained. Then, in order to examine the interaction of complainers and complainees, the same frequencies and crosstabulations were obtained for each group separately, eliminating from this stage of the analysis those tenants who had played other roles on the log. Finally, cross-tabulations of complaint log roles (complainer or complainee) by all social and architectural variables were obtained for the analysis of the differences between these two key groups.

In all, the data analyzed fell into five groups: all the management problem-tenants; problems excluding rules; the complaint log, all entries; the complainers; and the complainees. This corresponds to Figure 2.1 in Chapter 2, which outlined the general strategy to be undertaken in the analysis.

CODE BOOK FOR DATA ANALYSIS

Because of the importance of classification, grouping and coding decisions in the ultimate validity of any study, the complete coding scheme is included here.

Variable	Variable and Coding Description
1	Project (1, 2, 3, 4)
2	Race (1, 2, 3, 4, 5)
3	Age of head
4	Sex of head (1, 2)
5	Marital status (1, 2, 3, 4, 5)
6	Highest education (1, 2, 3, 4)
7	Total in family
8	Total minors
9	Total workers
10	Language (1, 2, 3, 4)
11	Years of occupancy
12	Gross family income
13	Major source of income (1, 2, 3, 4, 5, 6, 7, 8, 9)
14	Total teens
15	Teen boys
16	Primary problem (11, 12, 13, 21, 31, 32, 33, 34, 41, 42, 43, 44, 45, 46, 47, 51, 52, 53, 54, 55, 56, 61, 62, 71, 72, 81)
18	Secondary problem (11, 12, 13, 21, 31, 32, 33, 34, 41, 42, 43, 44, 45, 46, 47, 51, 52, 53, 54, 55, 56, 61, 62, 71, 72, 81)
19	Building height (1, 2)
20	Inner court (1, 2)
21	Apartment mix (1, 2, 3, 4, 5, 6)
22	First-floor apartment

Variable	Variable and Coding Description
23	Complaint log role (1, 2, 3, 4, 5, 6)
24	Development: (1—McCormack; 2—Charlestown; 3—South End; 4—Columbia Point)
25	Race (1—white; 2—nonwhite; 3—American Indian; 4—Spanish; 5—Oriental)
26	Age of head (15-29—young; 30-59—middle aged; 60-99—old)
27	Sex of head (1—female; 2—male)
28	Marital status (1—single; 2—married; 3—separated; 4—divorced; 5—widowed)
29	Highest education (1—elementary; 2—attended high school; 3—high school graduate; 4—attended college)
30	Total in family (1-3—small; 4-6—medium; 7-20—large)
31	Total minors (0-2—few; 3-4—medium; 5-20—many)
32	Total workers (1—none; 2-3—workers)
33	Language (1—english; 2—other)
34	Years in occupancy (1-5—5 or less; 6-10—6-10; 11-35—over 10)
35	Gross income (0-2500—low; 2501-4500—medium; 4501-20,000—high)
36	Main source of income (1—work; 2, 3, 4, 6, 8—public welfare; 5—Social Security; 7—veterans' benefits; 9—other)
37	Total teens (0—none; 1-2—some; 3-9—several)
38	Teen boys (0—none; 1-2—some; 3-9—several)
39	9-12 years olds (0—none; 1-2—some; 3-9—several)
40	Primary problem (11—animals; 12—failure to clean halls; 13—unauthorized persons; 21—chronic rent arrears; 31—senility or feebleness or health condition requiring special protection or services; 32—mental illness or retardation causing person to become problem to management; 33—alcohol-related; 34—child neglect; 41—theft via breaking and entering or handbag snatching; 42—physical assault; 43—sexual offenses; 44—intimidating gang activity; 45—narcotics; 46—child abuse or contributing to delinquency; 47—vandalism; 51—verbal harrassment of neighbors, passersby, staff; 52—conflict over care of public areas; 53—conflict over child control or rearing; 54—other types

Variable	Variable and Coding Description

of interpersonal conflicts including persons being harrassed; 55—racial or ethnic conflict; 56—chronic complaining; 61—housekeeping problems severe enough to concern neighbors or management; 62—sloppy disposal of refuse; 71—loud, disruptive noises, parties, music, machines, domestic quarrels, etc.; 72—uncontrolled child activity (more aggressive than 53); 81—multi-problem family, when in judgment of manager several of the above categories are combined in one outstanding family

Selected Variables 24-46 Recoded and Collapsed

25	Race (1—white; 2—nonwhite; 3-6—blank)
26	Age of head (15-39—young; 40-59—medium; 60-99—elderly)
28	Marital status (2—married; 1, 3, 4, 5—single if age less than 60)
29	Education (1, 2—less than high school graduate; 3, 4—high school graduate plus)
31	Total minors (small-medium—1-4; Large—5-20)
35	Gross family income (low—0-3499; high—3500-20,000)
36	Source (1—work; 2-8—benefit; 9—blank)
37	Total teens (0—none; 1-10—teens)
38	Teen boys (0—none; 1-10—teen boys)
39	9-12 year olds (0—none; 1-10—9-12 year olds)
40	Primary problem (administrative rule breaking—11, 12, 13, 21, 61, 62; health and aging—32, 32, 33, 34; interpersonal—46, 51, 52, 53, 54, 55, 56, 71, 72; severely disruptive or antisocial—41, 42, 43, 44, 45, 47, 81)
44	Apartment mix (1-2—small; 3-6—medium-large)
46	Complaint log (0—no; 1-5—yes)
41	Secondary problem (same as variable 41)
42	Building height (1—low; 2—high)
43	Inner court (1—inner; 2—street)
44	Apartment mix (1—small; 2—small and medium; 3—medium; 4—medium and large; 5—large; 6—small and large)

Variables	Variable and Coding Description
45	First floor (1—first; 2—upper)
46	Complaint log (0—no; 1—complainer; 2—complainee; 3—both; 4—subsequent; 5—anonymous)
47	Frequency (dummy)
48	Developments
49	Race (1—white; 2—nonwhite; 3-5—blank)
50	Age of head
51	Sex (less than 60)
52	Marital status (2—married; 1, 3, 4, 5—unmarried) less than 60
53	Highest education
54	Total in family
55	Total minors
56	Total workers
57	Language
58	Years in occupancy
59	Gross family income
60	Major source (1—work; 2—veterans' benefits; 3—Social Security; 4—OAA, APTD, AB; 5—AFDC; blank—GR and other) based on degree of stigma
61	Total teen
62	Teen boys
63	9-12 year olds
64	Problem type (1—11, 12, 22; 2—61, 62; 3—31, 32, 33; 4—51, 52, 53, 54, 55, 56; 5—71, 72; 6—81, 47, 43, 46; 7—41, 42, 44, 45) based on range of passivity to aggressivity
65	Building height
66	Inner court
67	Apartment mix (1-5) excluding large and small
68	Apartment mix (1-6) including large and small
69	First floor

NOTE

1. David J. Armor and Arthur S. Couch, The Data-Text Primer: An Introduction to Computerized Social Data Analysis Using the Data-Text System (New York: The Free Press, 1972).

Because the judgments of the managers in the four subject developments are so central to this study, it is important to review briefly the general orientation of each to his work and his views regarding the responsibility of management vis-à-vis the tenants. Further, it would be well to comment on the style of operation in each of the four offices, a factor that may have had some bearing on the kinds of problems that come to each manager's attention and on the quality of his relationship with the tenant body as a whole.

McCormack: The manager at McCormack is a white, middle-aged man of Irish ancestry with many years of experience at several levels in management. His ability to relate to tenants and his general competence on the job led to his appointment as manager in this development on November 18, 1970. Thus, with only six months in his current post at the time of the Phase II interview, he is the manager with the least time "in grade" and the least direct experience with his tenant group. Responsible for two large developments in South Boston, he spends most of his time away from the McCormack management office, where the pace is usually leisurely. With a majority of the McCormack units occupied by elderly families the atmosphere is remarkably serene. When an acute problem arises it is usually related to the illness of an elderly tenant and involves all the activities required in such a situation, such as obtaining medical services, notifying the next of kin, and arranging for ambulances, admission to hospitals or nursing homes. The manager feels highly responsible for the well-being of his tenants, particularly the elderly, and when social or health problems do arise he frequently becomes personally involved, even though there is a management aide on his staff whose job it is to handle them. He sees many of his problem tenants as simply persons who need to be protected and worried over, and he believes that this is, at least in part, his responsibility as manager.

The office itself is organized in a casual and open manner with only a partial partition between the public lobby area and the staff's work area. The manager's door is visible from the counter, and it is usually open. The assistant manager's desk is also in view and staff are easily accessible to tenants. The attitude of the secretarial and reception staff is informal, and many if not most tenants are recognized and addressed by name.

Charlestown: In Charlestown the manager has been on the job since January 28, 1970. Until then he had been director of personnel in the central BHA office for many years. He also is white, middle-aged, and of Irish background, and although he appears to be trying hard to do an efficient job of managing this aging development he makes no secret of his dislike for the assignment. While he expresses concern for the social and physical problems of many of his tenants, especially those who are being scapegoated by others, he seems preoccupied with his financial and physical maintenance responsibilities. Rent collection is an area of particular concern for him, as seen by the emphasis it received in his contribution to the problem-tenant typology. He is continually frustrated by the limitations on his authority—one example of which is the difficulty he has in dealing with unauthorized pets. He has a list of 106 complaints by tenants against dogs owned, contrary to Authority regulations, by other tenants. He states that if he were to pursue each of these complaints, after great expenditure of time, endless processing of papers, hearings, and finally days in court, he would be lucky to get rid of three dogs. He feels himself to be under constant pressure to perform tasks he has neither the power nor the resources to carry out. This is a theme that is not limited to this development or to this manager but that, nevertheless, seems more dominant in Charlestown than elsewhere.

The office is staffed by a mix of older long-time BHA employees and several younger newcomers to the organization. The result is an uneasy combination of the generally warm-hearted paternalism of the former and the "tenants' rights" orientation of the latter. Tenants can, at times, get caught in the crossfire or leave the office with contradictory impressions regarding their own rights and responsibilities in a given area. Physically the office is less open than McCormack, but the atmosphere is generally friendly and not forbidding.

South End: At the South End development the manager has been at his post since June 18, 1969. Before that he served as assistant manager and management aide in the same development, beginning in 1965. He is a black, middle-aged man who views the responsibilities of management in rather traditional terms, emphasizing attention to rent collections, maintenance problems, enforcement of rules, and staff discipline. He aspires to a high standard of housekeeping and public behavior for his tenants and has evidenced exasperation in the past toward social service workers who have failed to substantially alter the lifestyles of families whose performance as tenants he considered unsatisfactory. Whereas other managers frequently become involved in trying to find solutions to social problems that come to their attention, the manager at South End relies instead on quick referrals to police, hospitals, and social agencies.

The office is small and somewhat cramped, occupying what was originally designed as a two-bedroom apartment. Partly because of the spatial-organization factor, the office is quite closed, with the public lobby thoroughly fenced off from the staff working area by counters, the cashier's cage, and a locked gate. The manager's door is not visible from the reception area, and the attitude of the racially integrated front office staff is one of crisp and sometimes stern efficiency.

Columbia Point: The Columbia Point acting manager is a white, middle-aged woman whose training and experience has been in social service, group work, and community action agencies. She has been assistant manager at Columbia Point since January 28, 1971, and acting manager for several months since the serious illness of the manager. Even before then she was the principal management official to have direct contact with the tenant body. Her orientation to this job is in line with that of the softliners cited in Chapter 1, who viewed the public housing authority primarily as a social welfare agency. She has cultivated a network of relationships with social and health agencies in the community as well as with the police and sees her responsibility as including a concern for the social welfare of her tenants. Having a strong personal commitment to the notion of tenant rights, she has struggled to build an office staff that will be honestly responsive to tenant questions and problems.

The office atmosphere is lively and animated, with a mixture of ages, races, languages (a Puerto Rican management aide is a regular member of the staff and holds regular hours to deal with the problems of the growing number of Spanish-speaking tenants). There is a constant flow of tenants to and from the several staff offices, which, though physically removed from the public lobby, are made readily accessible through flexible operating procedures.

In the review of the tenant population this manager also discussed, in addition to the problem tenants of the moment, many other situations that had been problems previously, but that, through management intervention, had been solved satisfactorily. Twenty-eight in all, these consisted of elderly tenants who had complained of young children until given transfers to quieter buildings. Other cases involved families with financial difficulties and rent arrears problems, which were corrected by referral of the head of household to a successful employment opportunity. The manager speaks with pride of the fact that tenants with really serious problems tend to come to the management office for assistance—evidence that they see it as a place where there are concerned, helping people.

The managers did not contribute evenly to the problem-tenant typology; and, as stated in Chapter 4, the emphasis that they placed in their description of problem tenants in general was sometimes reflected in the kinds of specific problems they cited.

At McCormack the problems, listed in the same order in which they were given, were as follows:

1. alcoholism, especially among the elderly,
2. senility and deterioration of health,
3. lack of child control,
4. rent arrears,
5. hoodlums from outside the development hanging around in a menacing manner,
6. dogs,
7. hallways—arguments over cleaning,
8. mental illness when in an agitated state,
9. vandalism.

In Charlestown, a somewhat different constellation of problems was cited:

1. rent arrears,
2. disruptive behavior of certain problem families characterized by loud parties, fights, and so on,
3. teenage and preteen activity leading to noise, vandalism, and intimidation of the elderly,
4. senility leading to housekeeping problems, seclusion,
5. mental retardation and victimization of retarded individuals,
6. chronic complainers.

At South End the manager was unable to give as precise a list of problem types and seemed at first quite reluctant to concede that problems or problem tenants existed in his development. He did mention some conflicts between tenants, incidents in which some tenants had protested some of his policies, and that narcotics have been a problem in general to the neighborhood. He did, later, corroborate the suggestions made by the other managers as contained in the draft typology.

At Columbia Point the acting manager was particularly articulate and contributed much of the typology as it finally emerged.

Her career orientation and training had been in social work rather than housing management, and this is reflected in the emphasis in her list:

1. in general, behavior that is detrimental to the well-being of other tenants,
2. multi-problem families with several serious internal problems that make them disruptive to their neighbors,
3. animals that bother others,
4. nuisance behavior, such as loud noise and drunken parties,
5. verbal harrassment,
6. physical assault,
7. narcotics and related robberies,
8. vandalism, especially by preteens,
9. complainers,
10. mental illness, especially when in agitated state.

THE PROBLEM TENANT

The reader may recall the discussion in Chapter 1 of the general preoccupation with the multi-problem family on the part of housing management on both sides of the Atlantic. The importance placed upon this particular phenomenon in housing circles is unsupported by the information collected in this study (see Tables A.1 and A.2).

Of the 3,935 families in occupancy in the four target developments at the time of the interviews with managers, 196 or 4.5 percent were considered to be problem tenants. When those falling into the "rules" categories (most of which involved chronic nonpayment of rent) are omitted, the percentage drops to 3.4. The range between developments extended from 3.1 percent to 7.1 percent for all problem tenants and from 2.2 percent to 4.1 percent with "rules" omitted.

The importance of the rules group is uneven over developments. Thus, while rules represent up to 48.3 percent of the problem tenants identified in the South End development and 45.5 percent in Charlestown, their importance falls to 29.0 percent at McCormack and only 10.2 percent at Columbia Point.

The problem tenants whose characteristics place them in the "health" category represent the smallest group among the four general classifications. Only 14.3 percent of the total cases identified were health in nature. These consisted of eleven judged to be senile by their managers (four of these in McCormack, five at Columbia Point, and only one at Charlestown—a surprising fact in view of the high percentage of elderly-headed households there). Tenants judged to be mentally ill or alcoholic were listed in all developments except McCormack.

The largest general category, representing 33.2 percent of all problem tenants identified by managers, was that of "interpersonal problems." However, when the individual projects are examined, only at McCormack did it represent the highest general category (54.8 percent), while at Charlestown it trailed rules cases 39.0 percent to 45.5 percent, and in South End at 14.8 percent it followed both rules at 48.3 percent and severe disruption at 17.2 percent. At Columbia Point severe disruption made up 44.1 percent of the cases, while interpersonal problems of less severe nature accounted for only 23.7 percent of problem tenants cited. Those subcategories appearing most often consisted of chronic complaining, uncontrolled child behavior, and racial conflict. Charlestown contributed most

TABLE A.1

Distribution of Problem Tenants by Specific Problem Type

	All	McC	Chas	So E	Col
Total families (May 1971)	3935	1016	1118	506	1295
Total problem tenants	196	31	77	29	59
Percent of total families	4.9	3.1	7.1	5.7	4.5
Problem types:					
Administrative rules	64	9	35	14	5
Percent of total problems	32.7	29.0	45.5	48.3	10.2
Animals	8	4	2	1	1
Failure to clean halls	0	0	0	0	0
Unauthorized tenant	0	0	0	0	0
Rent arrears	53	5	31	13	4
Housekeeping	2	0	2	0	0
Sloppy waste disposal	0	0	0	0	0
Health	28	4	5	6	13
Percent of total problems	14.3	12.9	6.5	20.7	22.0
Senility	11	4	1	1	5
Mentally ill	8	0	1	3	4
Alcoholic	9	0	3	2	4
Child neglect	0	0	0	0	0
Interpersonal	65	17	30	4	14
Percent of total problems	33.2	54.8	39.0	13.8	23.7
Child abuse	1	0	1	0	0
Verbal harrassment	6	5	1	0	0
Conflict: hallways	0	0	2	0	0
Conflict: child handling	6	4	2	0	1
Person being harrassed	0	1	3	0	2
Racial conflict	12	2	8	0	2
Chronic complaining	15	3	5	2	5
Loud noises	6	2	1	1	2
Uncontrolled child	13	0	9	1	2
Severely disruptive	39	1	7	5	26
Percent of total problems	19.9	3.2	9.1	17.2	44.1
Multi-problem family	21	0	3	3	15
Theft	3	0	1	0	2
Assault	1	1	0	0	0
Sexual offenses	2	0	0	0	2
Intimidating gang activity	0	0	0	0	0
Narcotics	8	0	0	2	6
Vandalism (extreme cases)	4	0	3	0	1

Note: McC = McCormack; Chas = Charlestown; So E = South End; Col = Columbia Point. These abbreviations are used throughout this appendix.

TABLE A.2

Distribution of Problem Tenants by General Problem Types
("Rules" Excluded)

	All	McC	Chas	So E	Col
Total families (May 1971)	3935	1016	1118	606	1295
Number of problem tenants	132	22	42	15	53
Percent of total	3.4	2.2	3.9	3.0	4.1
By problem types:					
Health	28	4	5	6	13
Percent by project	21.2	18.1	11.8	40.0	24.5
Interpersonal	65	17	30	4	14
Percent by project	49.2	77.2	71.2	26.6	26.4
Severe disruption	39	1	7	5	26
Percent by project	29.4	4.5	16.6	33.3	49.0

of the uncontrolled child behavior and racial conflict cases. (Although the nonwhite population is a low 1 percent, it is still the most recently desegregated development.) Highest categories at McCormack were verbal harrassment and conflict about child handling. Interpersonal problems were only 13.8 percent at South End and only 23.7 percent at Columbia Point.

In each of the four developments there were problem types stressed by the manager that never appeared, either in the subsequent identification of problem tenants or in the complaint log. Some of these were problems that might, by their very nature, be difficult to ascribe to specific families, such as intimidating gang activity and sloppy waste disposal. Some were problems in which the offenders are almost invariably known, such as failure to clean the halls on assigned days, child neglect, or housing an unauthorized tenant. Other problems that figured highly in preliminary discussions appeared only once or twice among the identified problem tenants, among them assault, child abuse, and chronically bad housekeeping.

The proportion of severely disruptive tenants varies widely from project to project, with an overall average of 19.9 percent and a range from 3.2 percent at McCormack to 44.1 percent at Columbia Point. Columbia Point contributes 66.6 percent of all the cases included in this category. Among these are 15 of the total of 21 multiproblem families identified as problem tenants in the study and six of the eight cases of known involvement in narcotics.

In all, the families identified as multi-problem represented only 10.7 percent of all those considered by these four managers as problem tenants (and only .005 percent of all tenants in the target projects). Clearly, the multi-problem family does not figure highly as the source or the tenant-related problems of these managers. Even when the rules cases are omitted, the importance of the multi-problem family rises only to 15.6 percent of the problem-tenant population, a substantial level for a single problem classification but not high enough to justify the ubiquitous use of the multi-problem family concept as an explanation for all of management's problems.

THE COMPLAINT LOG

The complaint log was kept for ten weeks during which time there were a total of 61 entries across all four projects in which either the complainer, the complainee, or both were named. Anonymous complaints about general building conditions were not accepted unless at least one family was named in the complaint. In the 61 entries a total of 117 families were named in all roles. One hundred of these were in interacting pairs where both the complainee and complainer were named. There were only seven interaction situations that occurred more than once. These repeaters were counted only once for the statistical analysis, and for this reason more acceptable entries were recorded during the first week than in subsequent weeks (see Table A.3). In all, there were 25 entries at Columbia Point representing 47 tenant families, 18 entries at Charlestown representing 33 families, 9 at both McCormack and South End representing 16 and 21 families, respectively.

Table A.4 shows the types of problems expressed in the complaint log, a majority of which involved difficulties classified in the general category of interpersonal problems. Another large group (33.3 percent) consisted of severe disruption type problems, while rule breaking accounted for only 9.4 percent. None of the tenants appearing on the complaint log were involved in conflict that might be classified as having its roots in a health problem. The distribution of complaint-problem types among all family entries did not vary substantially among developments.

Fifty interacting pairs of families were identified on the log, distributed as shown in Table A.5. Distribution of problem categories by paired complaint incidents understandably did not vary substantially from the distribution among all appearances on the log, with interpersonal problems ranging from 43.7 percent at Columbia Point to 80 percent at South End and severe disruption ranging from 20 percent at McCormack and South End to 43.5 percent at Columbia Point.

AREAS OF OVERLAP

There was considerable overlap between those cases identified by the managers as problem tenants and those appearing in the complaint log: 23, or 11 percent, also appeared on the complaint log (see Table A.6). If one eliminates from the total those who were identified by the manager because of rule breaking behavior, as we shall in most of our analyses, the proportion of those appearing on the log rises to 17.3 percent. This percentage varies from a low proportion of overlap at Charlestown (9.5 percent of management's problem tenants), through South End (13.3 percent) and Columbia Point (18.5 percent), to a high at McCormack (27.3 percent).

Among those tenants who appeared both on the manager's list of problem tenants and upon the complaint log the distribution of problem types (as defined by the manager) differed somewhat from that found in the entire group of families appearing on the complaint log as defined by the complaining tenant (see Table A.7).

Families appeared on the list of problem tenants because the managers viewed them as problems; those appearing on the complaint

Weekly Entries on Complaint Log by Project

	Week Number										Total
	1 5/24–5/28	2 5/29–6/4	3 6/5–6/11	4 6/12–6/18	5 6/19–6/25	6 6/26–7/1	7 7/3–7/9	8 7/10–7/16	9 7/17–7/23	10 7/24–7/30	
All	12 (7)	5	8	6	9	12	5	2	0	2	61
McCormack	1 (1)	1	2	2	0	1	1	1	0	0	9
Charlestown	3 (1)	2	2	2	5	4	0	0	0	0	18
South End	2 (2)	0	2	1	1	3	0	0	0	2	9
Columbia Pt.	6 (3)	2	2	1	3	4	4	1	0	2	25

Note: Included are all entries in which complainer, complianee, or both were named. Numbers in parentheses indicate complaints that were to be repeated in future weeks.

TABLE A.4

Total of all Complaint Log Appearances by General Complaint Category

	All		McC		Chas		So E		Col	
	Number	Percent	Number	Percent	Number	Percent	Number	Percent	Number	Percent
All appearances	117	(100.0)	16	(13.7)	33	(28.2)	21	(17.9)	47	(40.2)
Rule breaking	11	(9.4)	3	(18.8)	2	(5.9)	0		6	(12.7)
Health	0		0		0		0		0	
Interpersonal	67	(57.3)	10	(62.5)	20	(60.6)	16	(76.2)	21	(44.7)
Severe disruption	39	(33.3)	3	(18.8)	11	(33.3)	5	(23.8)	20	(42.6)

TABLE A.5

Total of all Interacting Pairs Appearing on Complaint Logs
by General Complaint Category

	All	McC	Chas	So E	Col
All appearances	50	5	12	10	23
Rules	5	1	1	0	3
Health	0	0	0	0	0
Interpersonal	28	3	7	8	10
Severe disruption	17	1	4	2	10

TABLE A.6

Incidence of Complaint Log Appearances Among Problem Tenants
by Manager's General Problem Category

	All	McC	Chas	So E	Col
Total problem tenants	196	31	77	29	60
Number appearing on complaint log	23	6	4	2	10
Percent appearing on complaint log	11.6	19.4	5.2	6.9	16.7
Total problem tenants: administrative rules omitted	134	22	42	15	54
Number appearing on complaint log	23	6	4	2	10
Percent appearing on complaint log	17.2	27.3	9.5	13.3	18.5
Problem categories					
Number administrative rules	0	0	0	0	0
Number health	5	0	0	1	4
Number interpersonal	9	5	3	0	1
Number severely disruptive	8	1	1	1	5

TABLE A.7

Problem Tenants Appearing on Complaint Log by a Comparison
of Problem Category Perceptions by Managers and Tenants

Development	Total	Role on Log Complainer	Complainee	Manager-Tenant Agreement-Disagreement	Direction of Disagreement
All	22	7	14	A (4)	(-) 6
				D (4)	(+) 4
				D* (6)	
McCormack	6	2	4	A (1)	(-) 2
				D* (3)	(+) 1
Charlestown	3	1	2	A (2)	
South End	2	1	1	D (1)	(-) 1
Columbia Pt.	11	3	7	A (1)	
				D (3)	(-) 3
				D* (6)	(+) 4

Note: (+) = Tenants judge problem to be more serious than management. A = Agreement.
D = Disagreement, but compatible categories. D* = Disagreement, incompatible categories.

94

log did so because their neighbors viewed them as irritating, trouble-some, or threatening. When the same families appeared on both lists they frequently did so for different reasons. Of the 22 families appearing on both lists (a twenty-third family was initially included but later dropped because the entry was inappropriate) 14 were on the complaint log as complainees.

Of these 14 complainees there were four cases of complete agreement between manager and complaining tenant around both the general and specific categories of the problem. Four additional cases were in like or compatible categories (for example, a family, identified by the manager as a multi-problem family, that is complained against because of behavior that might be a function of the type assigned by the manager: uncontrolled child behavior, housekeeping problems, and so on.)

The remaining six cases represent clearer instances of dis-agreement. Three of these involved reaction to distinctive forms of behavior (verbal harrassment and vandalism, racial conflict and possession of an annoying dog, and theft and general nuisance) while the other three involved cases in which the manager perceived mental illness, senility, or alcoholism as a health problem whereas the tenants complained of specific behavior resulting from these conditions (verbal harrassment and assault). If the nine cases in which there was some disagreement of problem category are examined in terms of the direction of disagreement,* no clear pattern emerges. By using the degree of aggressivity discussed earlier as an index of seriousness, it is possible to determine direction from minus (less aggressive problems such as rule breaking) to plus (more aggressive problems such as severe disruption). In four of the nine cases of disagreement the tenants assign a more aggressive (plus) category and six a less aggressive (minus) one.

SPATIAL DISTRIBUTION OF DATA

Managers, when asked to indicate the areas in their develop-ments that they considered problem areas, outlined a total of 21 areas (see Table A.8), six in each of Charlestown and South End, five in McCormack, and four in Columbia Point. Five of these were cited

---

*The term direction here refers to the extent to which tenants judged a problem to be more or less serious than it had been judged by management. In Table A.7 the symbol (+) is used when tenants judge a problem to be more serious and (-) when they judge it to be less serious than does the manager.

TABLE A.8

Relationship of Problem Tenants and Tenant Complaints
to Problem Areas

Development	Areas	Presence of Clusters (3 or More) of Problem Tenants	Presence of Incidents of Tenant Complaints
McCormack	5	2	4
Charlestown	6	5	4
South End	6	1	1
Columbia Pt.	4	3	2
Total	21	11	11

because of the high incidence of vandalism; six were considered problem areas because of their use as "teenage hangouts" and the resultant noise and litter. Two involved proximity to a liquor store and the consequent attraction of derelicts to the area. High "wear and tear" was attributed in one case to the use of the area as a short-cut to a nearby shopping center, in another to the extreme high density of two high-rise buildings and the use of a courtyard as a preteen street-hockey area. In five areas the problems were attributed directly to very large, very disruptive, or very "filthy" families. In one instance the problem involved a continuing conflict between teen-agers in one building and elderly in another across the street.

Table A.8 shows the relationship of areas designated as problem areas by the managers to the location of non-rule-breaking problem tenants and incidents of conflict recorded on the complaint log. There are clusters of three or more problem tenants in only eleven of the 21 areas, while the remainder contain no such clusters. In five of the problem areas there are no problem tenants either within the area or immediately adjacent to it. Only at Charlestown is there a high correspondence between problem areas and problem tenants.

There was no apparent pattern in the mix of apartment sizes found in the problem areas. While large apartments and mixes of large and small figure in most of the Charlestown problem areas, this is not the case in the South End, where buildings with the large-small mix did not seem to present a problem, or at Columbia Point, where the buildings made up of large and medium-size apartments did not figure in any of the problem area designations.

The distribution of families appearing on the complaint log appears even less directly related to the problem areas. In ten of the areas, including the highest density buildings in the four developments, there were no families appearing on the complaint logs, while in eight others there was only one. In only three problem areas were there two or more complaint instances.

Thirty-two of the fifty complaints involving interacting pairs of families occurred within buildings, while the other eighteen were between buildings. Clustering was not related to building type in any of the developments.

ANALYSIS OF THE PROBLEM TENANT

The first major question posed by this study was, in effect, just who is the problem tenant and why is he a problem? The question was asked partly as a challenge to the popular conception of the problem tenant as identical to the problem family. On the basis of the findings presented above it can be stated that the tenants cited as problems by these four managers do not fit the traditionally accepted mold.

Buell found 2 to 3 percent of his sample to be multi-problem families; Willie and Weinandy and Geismar, when focusing on separate public housing developments, found 8 percent. If between 2 and 8 percent of the families in the four developments studied here were also multi-problem families, then only a small number of these went on to become problem tenants as well. Of all the problem tenants identified in this study only 21 were considered by the managers, using the criteria outlined in Chapter 4, to be multi-problem families. This represents only .53 percent of the total family population. If one were to consider only Columbia Point, where the manager is particularly attuned to family problems, the ratio rises to 15 out of the 1295 resident families, or 1.2 percent.

It is possible, of course, that many of those families falling into other categories might, in fact, have been identified as multi-problem if the managers had known more about them. Thus, if all those families cited for either severe disruption or interpersonal problems were for the moment redefined as multi-problem the proportion appearing among the problem tenants rises to 2.6 percent of the total population. This, however, would require a gross exaggeration of fragmentary evidence (for instance, making the parenting of an annoying child prima facie evidence of problem familyhood) and would be a misuse of the data. While the multi-problem-family category may, in fact, have failed to include all of those problem tenants that it might have, it represents a far smaller proportion of the problem tenants than might have been expected.

If 3 percent of the total population were, indeed, multi-problem families (a conservative estimate if Geismar, Willie, and Weinandy's findings were accurate and typical of public housing developments), and if being a multi-problem family led one irresistibly into the ranks of the problem tenants, then we might have expected 118 multi-problem families to be identified instead of the 21 that did appear. While multi-problem families represent a significant proportion of our problem tenant population (10 percent of all problem tenants and 16 percent if rule breaking is omitted), there are clearly many other ways in which a problem tenant can be identified.

Many problem tenants were classified as rule breakers, most of them due to chronic failure to pay rent. A few more were cited because of problems arising from particularly troublesome dogs. (Dog complaints in general were so numerous that managers and investigator agreed to cite only those cases that involved repeated offenses or especially alarming circumstances.) The importance a manager places upon this administrative category of problems seems to vary greatly and not in a way that can be logically attributed to the characteristics of the tenant population.

It is possible that the emphasis placed upon rule breaking categories in the list of problem tenants may be better attributable to the managers themselves and those aspects of their daily tasks that particularly interest or annoy them or appear to be most central to their responsibilities as they perceive them. While this study did not attempt to classify the managers in any precise manner, short vignettes are included in this appendix that may reflect the ways in which these four developments and their managers differed in their general styles of operation.

It was, in part, because of the disparity in the emphasis placed on rule breaking by the different managers that most of the analysis of problem tenants will be done with these rules cases omitted. Theoretical considerations are even more compelling. The study did not seek merely to describe the problem tenant as a composite picture drawn by the managers. Having done this, it hoped further to examine the identified problem population in terms of a range of social, economic, and architectural variables. While this design would not enable us to draw any firm conclusions regarding the causation of problem-tenanthood as a dependent variable, it was hoped that the analysis might point to certain social factors as being closely associated just as certain variables were earlier seen to be associated with the reputation of a development.

The hypotheses being explored in this study offer some suggestions regarding the possible causes of problem-tenanthood that arise from social behavior, but none really addresses such rule breaking problems as rent arrears. One exception to this might be a direct relationship between such factors as size and source of family income and payment of rent; however even this relationship is made cloudy by the large number of AFDC families whose rent is paid directly to the housing authority by the welfare department.

The following subsections will take up briefly those social variables in the problem-tenant population that, either because of their significance or their lack of it, may be important. Then, after a discussion of the correlation matrix produced by the reordering of variables on ordinal or interval scales, we will pass on to the complaint log and the whole issue of tenant interaction as a determinant of problem-tenant status.

Race

Table A.9 shows that the frequency of nonwhite* families appearing in the lists of problem tenants, either for all four developments or individual projects, does not differ meaningfully from that found in the overall population of the four target developments. However, if race is crossed with the three general categories of complaint, there is a significant difference in the way in which race is distributed (see Table A.10). We know that the elderly population is predominantly white; so the disproportionately large number of whites involved in problems categorized as health is not surprising. What is worthy of note is the high proportion of severe disruption problems recorded among nonwhite tenants. This appears to be almost entirely due to the identification at Columbia Point of five nonwhite families who have been involved in narcotics offenses, another two who have been implicated in local robberies, and two prostitutes identified as "sex" offenders. Interestingly, the multi-problem families at Columbia Point were more often white than nonwhite. (Eight were white while seven were nonwhite.)

One interesting negative finding relating to an ethnic rather than a racial variable concerned the role of Puerto Ricans in the developments. Puerto Ricans have been moving into Columbia Point in larger numbers in recent years, and South End has housed Spanish-speaking families for a decade. (1971 TSR figures show 90 Puerto Rican families at Columbia Point, 55 at South End, 10 at Charlestown, and none at McCormack.)[1] Although Puerto Rican friction with blacks and with whites has received considerable attention in the press, this group was conspicuously absent from the identified problem tenants.

---

*The term "nonwhite" is borrowed directly from the terminology of the Department of Housing and Urban Development as used in local housing authority census-taking.

TABLE A.9

Frequencies by Race in Total Population and Among Problem Tenants ("Rules" Omitted)

| | Nonwhite | | |
Development	Percent	Number	Totals
4 Target developments (1969)	21.5	816	3785
4 Targets: problem tenants	25.8	34	132
McCormack (1969)	3.0	28	991
McCormack: problem tenants	0.0	0	22
Charlestown (1969)	1.0	11	1118
Charlestown: problem tenants	3.2	2	42
South End (1969)	61.0	303	552
South End: problem tenants	60.0	9	15
Columbia Point (1969)	42.0	474	1124
Columbia Point: problem tenants	43.4	23	53

TABLE A.10

Crosstabulation: Problem Type by Race

| | White | | Nonwhite | |
	Number	Percent	Number	Percent
Health	21	(22.6)	5	(14.7)
Interpersonal	55	(59.1)	10	(29.4)
Severe disruption	17	(18.3)	19	(55.9)
Totals	93	(70.9)	34	(29.1)

Note: N + 131, X^2 = 17.29, p .001 with 2 df.

Only one Spanish surname appeared among all problem tenants at all developments—that at Columbia Point.

Age of Head of Household

In examining the age variable, we broke the adult age range from 20 to 99 into three categories: young, 20-39; medium, 40-59; and elderly, 60-99, paying particular attention to both ends of the range. As shown in Table A.11, the elderly tenants lived up to their reputations as ideal tenants in that their proportion among the problem-tenant population was lower than might have been expected. Younger families (heads between 20 and 39 years) appeared somewhat more frequently than their proportion in the population as a whole might have indicated, but the disparity is not so striking, with 38.1 percent of the problem families and 27.8 percent of the total population for the four developments falling into this group. This 10-point difference is largely a reflection of the higher proportions of younger problem tenants in the two developments with higher numbers of elderly at McCormack and Charlestown. At Columbia Point, with the largest number of problem tenants (N = 55), young persons represent 43.6 percent of the problem tenants and 39 percent of the total population.

When these age categories are crossed with the general types of problems, several clear patterns emerge, as shown in Table A.12. It is not surprising to find the elderly accounting for a greater proportion of the health-related problems in the sample, but the large proportion of younger families contributing to the severe disruption category is not so clear. The very large families that are often thought of as contributors to many of the more serious problems are usually headed by persons in the medium-age category. Here again, the explanation is in the Columbia Point contingent of severely disruptive tenants, which accounts for most of the weight in the young, severely disruptive cell. In the other developments medium-aged families are as well represented as the younger families in that problem category.

Sex of Head of Household

There is a disproportionate number of non-elderly, female-headed households in the problem-tenant group. While in the four developments as a whole single-parent households represent 33.5 percent, female-headed families are 63.3 percent of the problem tenants. This tendency is most striking at McCormack, where female-headed families constitute 54.5 percent of the problem tenants and

TABLE A.11

Frequencies by Age: Over 60 Years in Population
and Among Problem Tenants ("Rules" Omitted)

Population		Percent Over 60	Number Over 60	Totals
Total population:	4 target developments (1969)	40.8	1643	3785
Problem tenants:	4 targets, rules omitted	25.4	34	132
Total population:	McCormack (1969)	59.0	584	991
Problem tenants:	McCormack, rules omitted	22.7	5	13
Total population:	Charlestown (1969)	44.0	486	1118
Problem tenants:	Charlestown, rules omitted	26.2	11	31
Total population:	South End (1969)	36.0	184	552
Problem tenants:	South End, rules omitted	26.7	4	21
Total population:	Columbia Point (1969)	35.0	389	1124
Problem tenants:	Columbia Point, rules omitted	25.5	14	55

102

TABLE A.12

Crosstabulation: Problem Type by Age

	Young		Medium		Elderly	
	Number	Percent	Number	Percent	Number	Percent
Health	5	(9.8)	11	(22.4)	12	(36.4)
Interpersonal	23	(45.1)	25	(51.0)	17	(51.5)
Severe disruption	23	(45.1)	13	(26.5)	4	(12.1)
Total	51	(38.3)	49	(36.8)	33	(24.9)

Note: $N = 133$; $X^2 = 14.596$; $p < .006$ with 4 df.

only 25 percent of the total population, and least impressive at Columbia Point where they are 65.2 percent of the problem tenants and 55 percent of the total population.

When the sex of the non-elderly heads of household is crossed with problem type, there is little of note that is statistically significant. The distribution of frequencies is approximately what might be expected if the cells had been filled at random, except for the scarcity of units appearing in the health category row, which might have been anticipated in view of the concentration of health problems among the elderly. This, of course, was true for male-headed as well as female-headed households.

Family Size and Composition

In Table A.13 family size is examined in terms of the frequency of large families (seven or more members). When family size is crossed with problem type, there proves to be a significant association between the two. In this step families were divided into three groups—small (1 to 3 members), medium (4 to 6 members), and large (7 or more members)—and crossed with the general problem categories (Table A.14).

Once again, this result was made possible largely by the fact that small and, presumably, elderly families account for 22 of the 28 cases of health problems while the larger families account for only 4. The importance of family size in relationship to severely disruptive problems is less clear, in that there are almost as many (although a smaller proportion of) small families identified as

103

TABLE A.13

Frequencies by Family Size in Total Population
and Among Problem Tenants ("Rules" Omitted)

Population	Percent 7 Members or More	7 Members or More	Total
Total population: 4 target developments (1969)	10.4	395	3785
Problem tenants: 4 targets, rules omitted	24.8	33	132
Total population: McCormack (1969)	4.0	47	991
Problem tenants: McCormack, rules omitted	9.1	2	22
Total population: Charlestown (1969)	8.0	92	1118
Problem tenants: Charlestown, rules omitted	26.2	11	31
Total population: South End (1969)	8.0	40	552
Problem tenants: South End, rules omitted	13.3	2	15
Total population: Columbia Point (1969)	19.0	216	1124
Problem tenants: Columbia Point, rules omitted	33.3	18	54

severely disruptive as there are larger families so identified. At
Columbia Point, where the crossed variables failed to achieve a level
of significance above p = .278 (with four degrees of freedom), there
were as many small families identified as severely disruptive as
there were small families in the health category.

The association between such factors as the presence of teen-
agers of preteenagers and the type of problem manifested is more
difficult to assess because information on these variables is not
available in adaptable form for the population as a whole. In the
problem-tenant population the proportion of families with teenage
children ranges between 36.8 percent and 47.5 percent in all developments except the South End, where it slipped to only 26.7 percent.
A similar picture is seen when families with preteen children (from
9 to 12 years of age) are considered. Families in this group make
up from 31.0 percent to 50.8 percent of the problem-tenant population,
with the exception, once again, of the South End where the proportion
is only 26.7 percent. When the teenage child variable is crossed
with the problem categories for all four target developments there
is an association at a high level of significance (see Table A.15).
This result would appear to be attributable primarily to the relatively
small number of health problems and the larger proportion of severe
disruption problems present among the families who have teenage
children. This association holds up when individual developments
are examined but at less significant levels (from .158 at McCormack
to .074 at Columbia Point, both with 2 df).

If families with preteenage children are crossed in the same
manner with problem types, an identical pattern emerges, with a
small number of health problems and a somewhat larger proportion
of severe disruption problems among this group. These results are
only what might have been expected in view of the increased incidence

TABLE A.14

Crosstabulation: Size of Family by Problem Category

	Small		Medium		Large	
	Number	Percent	Number	Percent	Number	Percent
Health	22	(34.4)	2	(5.7)	4	(12.1)
Interpersonal	29	(45.3)	21	(60.0)	15	(45.5)
Severe						
disruption	13	(20.3)	12	(34.3)	14	(42.4)
Total	64	(48.5)	35	(26.5)	33	(25.0)

Note: N = 132; X^2 = 15.56; p < .004 with 4 df.

105

TABLE A.15

Crosstabulation: Teenage Children by Problem Category

	None		Teens	
	Number	Percent	Number	Percent
Health	24	(31.7)	4	(7.0)
Interpersonal	36	(47.4)	29	(50.9)
Severe disruption	16	(21.1)	24	(42.1)
Total	76	(57.1)	57	(42.9)

Note: $N = 133$; $X^2 = 14.215$; $p. = .001$ with 2 df.

of health problems among the elderly (who usually have no children residing with them) and the role played by children in many of the problem types that make up the severe disruption category (vandalism: involvement in narcotics insofar as it is a youth-associated phenomenon; prevalent forms of theft such as handbag snatching; and multiproblem families that usually include at least some children).

Sources of Income

Information on source of income is available in two forms: the number of persons in each household who are employed, and whether or not the principal source of income is employment or some form of public transfer payment, such as public assistance or Social Security. While most tenants fall into one or the other of these groups, there is an overlapping area of about 5 percent in which some family members are employed, while the major source of incomes remains transfer payment.

In the overall population of the four target developments 71 percent of the families receive their income primarily from transfer payments, and this proportion does not change markedly when one looks at the problem tenants. The only variance between source of income figures for the total population and for the problem tenants occurs at McCormack, where the proportion of families receiving transfer payments is 10 percent less among problem tenants than in the overall project population (54 percent instead of 64 percent). At Charlestown the picture is reversed, with transfer-payment families making up 61 percent of the population and 82.9 percent of the problem tenants. The size of the decrease at McCormack is

106

largely due to the statistical effect of a few employed problem tenants upon a relatively small number of cases. In addition, the bulk of the families on transfer payments at McCormack are elderly; and, as noted above, this group doesn't appear with great regularity among the problem tenants. The increase at Charlestown is less easily explained. There AFDC families do appear among the problem families with greater regularity, while problem families with employed members fall to a low of 14.3 percent.

Table A.16 shows that families with employed members represent a smaller proportion of the problem tenants than they do of the entire population. Yet, as earlier was discussed, the differences are not so striking as to offer much support to the Starr position regarding the undesirability of dependent families. This becomes especially apparent when the employment variable is crossed with the problem type. With all four developments considered there is no indication that the two variables are associated (X^2 = .983, insignificant) or that having no employed person in a family is related to a more serious category of problem. Taken individually, each development yields a like result.

Transiency

Tables A.17 and A.18 show frequencies by years of occupancy. Families with fewer years in occupancy appear in greater numbers among the problem tenants than their proportion in the entire population would indicate, both for the four developments as a group and for three of the four taken individually. Only at McCormack is the pattern reversed. A mirror image of this is seen when the frequencies of occupancy over ten years are examined, except at McCormack and Charlestown, where the older occupants represent a slightly higher percentage of the problem families than they do in the total population.

The first of these patterns appear to be the stronger and, except for McCormack, there seems a greater likelihood that newly arrived families will become problem tenants, nevertheless. At both McCormack and Charlestown there are a small group of long-time residents who have been chronic problems.

Architectural Features

Comparisons of frequencies of architectural variables as they occur in the design of the developments and in residences of problem tenants was a discouraging exercise. In comparing the proportion

TABLE A.16

Frequencies by Families with Employed Member in Total Population and Among Problem Tenants ("Rules" Omitted)

Population	Percent with Workers	Number with Workers	Total
Total population: 4 target developments (1969)	33.0	1263	3785
Problem tenants: 4 targets, rules omitted	20.1	27	132
Total population: McCormack (1969)	38.0	379	991
Problem tenants: McCormack, rules omitted	31.8	7	22
Total population: Charlestown (1969)	38.0	425	1118
Problem tenants: Charlestown, rules omitted	14.3	6	42
Total population: South End (1969)	33.0	171	552
Problem tenants: South End, rules omitted	20.0	3	15
Total population: Columbia Point (1969)	25.0	288	1124
Problem tenants: Columbia Point, rules omitted	20.0	11	55

TABLE A.17

Frequencies by Years in Occupancy: 5 or Less in Total Population and Among Problem Tenants ("Rules" Omitted)

Population	Percent 5 Years or Less	Number 5 Years or Less	Total
Total population: 4 target developments (1969)	34.0	1298	3785
Problem tenants: 4 targets, rules omitted	48.5	64	132
Total population: McCormack (1969)	27.0	263	991
Problem tenants: McCormack, rules omitted	18.2	4	22
Total population: Charlestown (1969)	33.0	362	1118
Problem tenants: Charlestown, rules omitted	45.2	19	42
Total population: South End (1969)	39.0	197	552
Problem tenants: South End, rules omitted	40.0	6	21
Total population: Columbia Point (1969)	42.0	477	1124
Problem tenants: Columbia Point, rules omitted	66.0	35	53

TABLE A.18

Frequencies by Years in Occupancy: 10 or More in Total Population
and Among Problem Tenants ("Rules" Omitted)

Population	Percent Ten Years or More	Number Ten Years or More	Total
Total population: 4 target developments (1969)	38.0	1450	3785
Problem tenants: 4 targets, rules omitted	30.0	40	132
Total population: McCormack (1969)	51.0	518	991
Problem tenants: McCormack, rules omitted	68.2	15	13
Total population: Charlestown (1969)	43.0	467	1118
Problem tenants: Charlestown, rules omitted	45.2	14	42
Total population: South End (1969)	36.0	182	552
Problem tenants: South End, rules omitted	33.3	5	15
Total population: Columbia Point (1969)	25.0	283	1124
Problem tenants: Columbia Point, rules omitted	11.3	6	53

of apartments in elevator (high-rise) buildings with the proportion of
problem tenants residing in those buildings, one finds a difference of
24 percent at South End; but this is accounted for almost entirely by
the fact that the tower in the center of that development is made up
of small apartments now occupied exclusively by elderly tenants (who
represent a small proportion of the problem tenants at that development). At Columbia Point the only other development with a mixture
of high- and low-rise apartment buildings, there is only a 5.3 percent
difference between the overall proportion of high-rise apartments
incorporated in the design and the proportion of problem tenants
occupying them—78.0 percent and 72.7 percent respectively.

Inner-court entrance occur in the designs of all of the target
developments except Columbia Point. In the two low-rise developments
McCormack and Charlestown, problem tenants occupy inner-court
residences in proportions 18.9 percent and 17.7 percent higher than
the design itself would have led us to anticipate. At South End, a
partially high-rise project, this pattern was reversed but in lesser
magnitude. When the incidences of problem-tenant identification were
examined in terms of the type of problem being expressed, there
appeared to be no significant relationship between inner-court
entrances and the type of problem occurring. Thus expectations that
inner-court entrances might be more conducive to interactive types
of problems as opposed to health-related difficulties were not realized.

Table A.19 shows the frequencies of medium and large apartment sizes as they appear in the target developments and as residences
of problem tenants. Although frequency of medium and large apartments does not seem, when all four developments are considered
together, to be unduly associated with the presence of problem tenants,
when we compare individual developments there are quite different
relationships in each of the four locations. At McCormack problem
tenants in medium and large apartments represent a far larger
proportion of the problem-tenant population than units of that type
represent in the design of the development. On the other hand, at
Charlestown and the South End the picture is reversed. Only at
Columbia Point do the proportions come within 10 percent of one
another, and this accounts for the small differences when all four
are taken as a group.

Occupancy of a first-floor apartment does not appear to be
related to identity as a problem tenant. In the four developments
first-floor apartments represent 25 percent of the units and 35.7
percent of the problem tenants. In every individual project the
problem tenants occupy first-floor apartments in a slightly larger
proportion than such apartments represent in the design of the
developments, but nowhere is the difference more than 13 percent.
When crossed with the problem categories there is no significant

TABLE A.19

Frequencies by Apartment Size (Medium and Large) in Total Population and Among Problem Tenants ("Rules" Omitted)

Population	Percent Three to Six Bedrooms	Number Three to Six Bedrooms	Total
Total population: 4 target developments (1969)	48.0	1817	3785
Problem tenants: 4 targets, rules omitted	52.2	70	134
Total population: McCormack (1969)	20.0	198	991
Problem tenants: McCormack, rules omitted	54.5	12	22
Total population: Charlestown (1969)	82.0	916	1118
Problem tenants: Charlestown, rules omitted	59.5	25	42
Total population: South End (1969)	36.0	199	552
Problem tenants: South End, rules omitted	13.3	2	15
Total population: Columbia Point (1969)	47.0	528	1124
Problem tenants: Columbia Point, rules omitted	13.3	31	15

relationship to report, with first-floor occupancy seemingly unassociated with the type of problem cited by the managers (X^2 = 1.804, significant at p = .406 with 2 df). It should be noted, however, that first-floor occupancy did seem to have some bearing on the role that a tenant played on the complaint log. This will be discussed in more detail below.

Correlations of Social and Architectural Variables with Aggressivity of Problem

When the variables were converted to ordinal scale and correlated with the problem type ordered in terms of the degree of aggressivity expressed, several of the relationships already revealed in the tests of association reappeared (see Table A.20).

Aggressivity correlated most highly with race (positively) and age of head of household (negatively); also significant, but at a lower level, were the correlations with the reputation of the development and the major source of income.

The high positive correlation of aggressivity of problem type with race (nonwhite) is, once again, attributable to several severe disruption cases at Columbia Point. This correlation holds at Columbia Point even when only non-elderly cases are considered (r = .551). It should be noted, however, that the crimes incorporated in the most aggressive categories included some activities that might be considered "crimes without victims" (such as prostitution or dealing in narcotics), which do not involve directly assaultive behavior and often are more destructive to the offender than to others. This type of activity can be problematic to management and damaging to the whole social fabric, but the fact that it is not "violent" behavior should be kept in mind in interpreting these findings.

The correlation with age is negative, as might be expected, with the elderly rarely involved in problems that would have been categorized as severe. Family size, as suggested in the previous analysis, was highly correlated with aggressivity of problem, but only at Charlestown and Columbia Point.

That the reputation score of the development was correlated with aggressivity might lend some credence to either the notion that the stereotype of a poor reputation leads to the labeling of more families as problem tenants or, conversely, the notion that project reputation is a reflection of the character of tenant behavior that comes to the attention of management. The correlation with source of income indicates some relationship between aggressivity of behavior and degree of dependency (source of income scaled from work through Social Security and pension to dependency upon public assistance,

TABLE A.20

Correlation Coefficients: Social and Architectural Variables
by Aggressivity of Problem ("Rules" Omitted)

Variable	All Developments	McC	Chas	So E	Col
Developments (reputation)	.247^b	—	—	—	—
Race	.349^c	.000	-.119	.114	.513^c
Age	-.381^c	-.521^a	-.373^a	-.235	-.412^b
Sex of head	-.112	-.440	-.009	.050	-.089
Marital status of head	.070	.440	.079	.346	-.143
Highest education	.030	.176	.356^a	-.020	-.098
Total in family	.314^c	-.025	.390^a	.447	.309^a
Total minors	.307^c	.354	.342^a	.447	.309^a
Total workers	.036	.062	.129	-.165	.112
Language	-.044	.000	-.083	.261	-.129
Years in occupancy	-.184^a	-.309	.070	.204	-.055
Gross family income	.178^a	.039	.422^b	.044	.198
Major source of income	.238^b	.226	.005	.375	.287^a
Total teenagers	.279^b	.038	.373^a	.064	.297^a
Teenage boys	.177^a	.068	.160	.067	.211
9-12 year olds	.288^c	.417	.265	.323	.237
Building height	.082	—	—	-.126	.144
Inner-court	.192^a	.158	.043	.345	—
Apartment mix (type 1-5)	.236^a	.272	.205	-.244	.187
Apartment mix (type 1-6)	.199^a	.272	.263	-.006	.187
First-floor	.042	.158	-.104	.534*	-.027

^{a}Significant at least .05 level.
^{b}Significant at least .01 level.
^{c}Significant at least .001 level.

113

ending with the most maligned category, AFDC). It is probable, however, that the effect of age and the size of family as distributed among these income-source types is a major influence here.

That certain variables did not correlate highly with aggressivity of problem is also interesting. Sex of the head of household did not seem to be related to the type of problem expressed, nor did the marital status of the head, the highest education of the head, or total workers (thus neutralizing the otherwise significant level of correlation for source of income).

TARGET DEVELOPMENTS COMPARED

Just as the survey of the social characteristics of the twenty-five family developments in Boston revealed that there was no typical housing development, this review of the distribution of social variables among problem tenants in relation to the frequencies found in the entire populations failed to yield a typical problem-tenant profile. Table A.21 shows the relationship of the frequency of various social variables as they occur among problem tenants and among total populations.

In only two cases, race and sex of head, is there any uniformity of findings across all developments; and only at Charlestown is there a combination of variables that appears in disproportionate measure among the problem tenants, namely, large families, economically dependent upon transfer payments, who have been in residency five years or less. The combination of large families with five or fewer years in residency also occurs at Columbia Point, but there is no disproportionate share of problem tenants among those families who are economically dependent. The predicted scarcity of problem tenants who are employed only materialized at Charlestown and South End.

The developments that represent the greatest differences in terms of the characteristics of their problem tenants were McCormack and Columbia Point, and these differed most in their demographic characteristics as well. It was these two developments that also occupied opposite ends of the Reputation Scale in our sample.

McCormack's problem tenants differed from the overall population in that they presented a higher proportion of younger heads of household, of female-headed households, and (unexpectedly) of tenants with ten years or more in residence. Elderly tenants represented a smaller proportion than in the total population. This group, altogether, constituted only 2.2 percent of the tenant families and were involved mainly in interpersonal problems (17 cases, or 77.2 percent of all problems cited). Only one problem was classified as severely disruptive.

114

TABLE A.21

Relationship of Frequencies of Social Variables Among
Problem Tenants to Frequencies Among Total
Tenant Populations, by Development

	McC	Chas	So E	Col
Race				
(percent nonwhite)	0	0	0	0
Elderly head				
(percent over 60)	—	—	0	0
Young head				
(percent 20-39)	+	0	0	0
Sex of head				
(percent female)	+	+	+	+
Large family				
(percent 7 or more)	0	+	0	+
Workers present	0	—	—	0
Income from				
transfers	0	+	0	+
5 Years occupancy				
or less	0	+	0	+
10 Years occupancy				
or more	+	0	0	—

Note: 0 = difference of less than 10 percent between frequency among problem tenants and among total population. + or - = direction of difference with plus equal to a frequency among problem tenants 10 percent or more greater than that found in total population.

On the other hand, at Columbia Point the problem tenants differed from the overall population in that they included a higher proportion of larger families, female-headed households, families with occupancy of five years or less, and families receiving their income from some form of public transfer payment. This group made up a far higher proportion (53 cases or 4.1 percent) of the tenant families than expected and was involved mainly in problems classified as severely disruptive (26 cases or 49.0 percent).

Thus, as reputation fell, both the number and severity of the problems cited rose, these problems occurring to a disproportionate extent among younger, larger, economically dependent families of rather recent tenure. However—and this is important—while these variables occur among problem tenants at disproportionate levels within the low-reputation developments, problem tenants of all types continue to make up a relatively small proportion of the total population. Thus, for example, while 18 of Columbia Point's large families account for 33.3 percent of its problem-tenant population, they still represent only eight percent of all the large families.

TENANT INTERACTION AS REFLECTED IN THE COMPLAINT LOG

One major proposition posed by this study is that conflict between neighbors based upon differences along several social variables is a factor strongly associated with the identification of families that are problem tenants to management. To verify whether or not this is, indeed, the case, we must first show that there is a greater association between intertenant conflict as reflected in entries on the complaint log and whether or not a family is a problem tenant than would be true if the problem tenants were randomly selected. Once this has been done, it will be necessary to ask whether complaints to the management about certain families are not, in fact, based upon behavior that might be considered deviant rather than rooted in social differences as suggested here. If there are significant differences between those making the complaints (the complainers) and those being complained about (the complainees), then the second proposition will be supported, at least in relation to those variables along which there are true differences. If there are no significant differences, it will be necessary to concede that it is either really deviant behavior that is the basis of the intertenant conflict or other factors that were beyond the purview of this study. An assumption in this analysis is that overt behavioral deviance is distributed randomly throughout the population rather than associated uniquely with certain social variables.

The area of overlap between problem tenants and tenants appearing on the complaint log (including all roles) was examined in relation to the total population and the total number of entries on the complaint log. Using the test for the Standard Error of Proportions,* we asked whether the proportion of problem tenants appearing on the complaint log was significantly different from the proportion of problem tenants in the population. A difference, significant at $p = .0001$, was found for all four target developments taken as a group and for individual developments with the exception of South End,

---

*$Z_{sp} = \dfrac{P-P}{PQ/n}$

where there was no significant difference, and Charlestown, where the level of significance was lower (p = .01). Thus, except at South End, if a family is considered a problem tenant by the manager there is a high probability that they will also appear on the complaint log. Family interaction, then, can be accepted in three out of four developments as a major factor in the determination of family's identification as a problem tenant.

COMPLAINERS AND COMPLAINEES COMPARED

The final and most critical step in the analysis of this data was the crosstabulation of the role played by a tenant on the complaint log with the social and architectural variables already discussed. Here the analysis is limited to pairs of complainers and complainees, thus omitting cases that appeared on the log as the subject of anonymous complaints or as complainers against anonymous parties. The results were discouraging in their clarity. There was little evidence of real differences between complainers and complainees when crossed with any of the variables, although some relationships were less significant than others.

Race was associated with complaint-log role at an insignificant level (X^2 = 1.172; p = .279 with 1 df when all four developments are considered together); but this alone means little because of the uneven distribution of nonwhites among developments. Perhaps the only association of race and role worth reporting is that found at Columbia Point. Here it was the imbalance of whites and blacks among the complainers that accounted for the difference, with whites playing the role of complainer 18 out of 22 times. When the incidents of conflict are examined case by case at Columbia Point this association of race and complaint log role becomes less significant. Of all 23 complaint instances 16 involved an interaction of whites with whites or of blacks with blacks. Only 7 involved black-white interaction. That these were all one way (white complaining against black) accounts for the significant finding reported in Table A.22.

When role is crossed with age (young-medium-elderly) there is no association worth reporting nor any evidence that the expected phenomenon of elderly tenants complaining about young families is actually occurring. On the contrary, in the development with the largest proportion of elderly tenants (McCormack), there is not a single elderly tenant appearing on the log as part of a pair. (Two did appear on the log complaining about unknown persons.) At Columbia Point 17 of the instances of complaint occurred within age categories (young with young, middle-aged with middle-aged, elderly with elderly). Only six involved interaction across categories, and five of these were young with middle-aged.

117

TABLE A.22

Crosstabulation: Complaint Log Role by Race, Columbia Point

	White		Nonwhite		
--	Number	Percent	Number	Percent	Total
Complainer	18	(62.1)	4	(28.6)	22
Complainee	11	(37.9)	10	(71.4)	21
Total	29	(67.4)	14	(32.6)	43
					(1 blank)

Note: $X^2 = 3.005$, $p = 0.84$ with 1 df.

The sex of the head of household, a favorite variable among the group referred to earlier as the new pessimists, proved to be unrelated to roles on the complaint log ($X^2 = .501$ for the four target developments, significant at $p = .479$ with 1 degree of freedom). Only at Charlestown was there any difference in the distribution of roles with female-headed households representing 10 out of 12 complainees and only half of the complainers (Fisher's Exact Test = .097; significant at $p = .097$).

The most statistically significant relationship encountered in this analysis was that resulting from the crosstabulation of role with educational attainment of the head of household (see Table A.23). However, this pattern held only when the four projects were grouped. Singly, the relationship of education and complaint-log role did not prove to be significant.

TABLE A.23

Crosstabulation: Complaint Log Role by Education

	High School		High School Grade		
--	Number	Percent	Number	Percent	Total
Complainer	37	(57.8)	12	(35.3)	49
Complainee	27	(42.2)	22	(64.7)	49
Total	64	(63.2)	34	(36.8)	98

Note: X^2 (Yates) = 3.648; $p = .057$ with 1 df.

118

Crosstabulation: Complaint Log Role by Source of Income

| | Transfer Payments | | Work | | |
	Number	Percent	Number	Percent	Total
Complainer	38	(53.5)	6	(35.3)	44
Complainee	33	(46.5)	11	(64.7)	44
Total	71	(79.5)	17	(20.5)	88

Note: X^2_{Yates} = 1.167, p = .280 with 1 df.

Another interesting negative finding was the lack of difference in the roles played on the complaint log by families of different sizes. For all developments grouped there is no significant association between family size and role, nor is there for any of the individual developments. Expectations that families of different sizes living in proximity (and most complainer-complainee pairs shared the same stairwell) would be in conflict was not borne out by the data (X^2 = 2.814, significant at p = .245 with 2 degrees of freedom). Not only was there no relationship of these variables in the aggregate, but a pair-by-pair examination of the logs indicated that, for the most part, families were complaining about other families of like size. Other variables related to family size (number of minors, teens, and preteens) yielded similar negative results when crossed with complaint-log role (X^2_{Yates} = .654, significant at p = .419 with 1 df; X^2_{Yates} = 1.488, significant at p = .223 with 1 df; and X^2_{Yates} = 0.000, significant at p = .5 with 1 df, respectively).

Number of years in occupancy does not seem to have an important bearing upon the role a tenant plays in intertenant conflict as reflected on the complaint log. Short-timers and old-timers each are evenly distributed between complainer and complainee, and the cross statistics for these two variables yield insignificant results (X^2 = 1.238 for four target developments, significant at p = .5 with 2 degrees of freedom). Similar results were found in each of the individual developments. Nowhere did the expected pattern of older residents complaining about newcomers emerge.

Our final social variable crossed with complaint log role was source of income, another favorite among the new pessimists. Interestingly, the cross statistic in this case also was significant at a very low level (see Table A.24). There was no pattern of working families complaining against those receiving welfare payments; rather most of the activity on the log reflected those receiving public benefits and transfer payments complaining against each other. Working families were, if anything, underrepresented in the complainer category.

The architectural variables were, perhaps, the most fruitless group of all. This was primarily because pairs appearing on the complaint log will usually share like architectural characteristics in that they, in most cases, occupy the same building. Thus, cross-tabulations for the four target developments yielded insignificant results for building height, inner-court entry, and apartment size. First-floor entries show a slight level of association with complaint log role (X^2_{Yates} = 2.339, significant at p = .127 with 1 degree of freedom). This is caused by an uneven distribution of first-floor apartments between complainer and complainee roles: twice as many of the first-floor entries appear as residences of complainees than of complainers. This is a reversal of the pattern that might have been expected. Instead of first-floor apartment dwellers, living as they do near the busy and often noisy front door, complaining about the child traffic, and so on, they appear more often to be the subjects of complaint from persons on the upper floors.

NOTE

1. Maureen Power, Analysis of Boston Housing Authority Tenant Status Review, 1971, with totals based on a 5 percent sample. Mimeographed paper circulated at Brandeis University, Waltham, Massachusetts, 1972.

BOOKS AND PERIODICALS

Abrams, Charles. The City is the Frontier. New York: Harper and Row, 1965.

Alexander, Christopher. "The City as a Mechanism for Sustaining Human Contact." Environment for Man. Edited by William Ewald, Jr. Bloomington: Indiana University Press, 1967.

Altschuler, Alan. The City Planning Process. New York: Cornell University Press, 1965.

Banfield, Edward. The Unheavenly City: The Nature and Future of Our Urban Crisis. Boston: Little, Brown and Co., 1968.

Bauer, Catherine. "The Dreary Deadlock of Public Housing." Architectural Forum, May 1957, p. 140.

_____ "Social Questions in Housing and Community Planning." Journal of Social Issues 7, nos. 1 and 2 (1951).

Becker, Howard S. The Outsiders: Studies in the Sociology of Deviance. New York: Macmillan Co., 1963.

Bellin, Seymour, and Louis Kriesberg. Residential Areas as a Locus of Behavior Influence. Mimeographed. Syracuse, N.Y., 1965

Berger, Peter L., and Thomas Luckman. The Social Construction of Reality. Garden City, N.J.: Doubleday and Co., 1967.

Beyer, Glen H. Housing: A Factual Analysis. New York: Macmillan Co., 1958.

_____ . Housing and Society. New York: Macmillan Co., 1965.

Bitner, Egon. "The Police on Skid Row: A Study of Peace Keeping." American Sociological Review, October 1967.

Boer, Albert. The Community Service Center. Boston: United South End Settlements, 1961.

Buell, Bradley, and Associates. Community Planning for Human Services. New York: Columbia University Press, 1952.

Cronbach, L. S. "Test Reliability." Psychometrics no. 12 (1947); no. 16 (1951).

Davis, James A., Joe L. Spaeth, and Carolyn Huson. "A Technique for Analyzing the Effect of Group Composition." American Sociological Review, April 1961.

Deutscher, Irwin. "The Gatekeeper in Public Housing." Among the People: Encounters with the Poor. Edited by Irwin Deutscher and Elizabeth J. Thompson. New York: Basic Books, 1968.

Filker, David. "Public Housing Management Must Accept Family Rehabilitation Responsibility." Journal of Housing, May 1956.

Festinger, Leon, Stanley Schacter, and Kurt Bock. Social Pressure in Informal Groups: A Study of Human Factors in Housing. New York: Harper, 1950.

Freedman, Leonard. Public Housing: The Politics of Poverty. New York: Holt, Rinehart and Winston, 1969.

Gamson, William. Power and Discontent. Homewood, Illinois: The Dorsey Press, 1968.

Gans, Herbert. "Planning and Social Life: Friendship and Neighbor Relations in Suburban Communities." Journal of the American Institute of Planners, May 1961.

_____. The Urban Villagers: Group and Class in the Lives of Italian-Americans. Glencoe, Illinois: The Free Press, 1962.

_____. The Levittowners. New York: Random House, 1967.

Geismar, L., and Louis Kriesberg. The Forgotten Neighborhood. Metuchen, New York: Scarecrow Press, 1967.

_____, and M. LaSorte. Understanding the Multi-Problem Family. New York: Association Press, 1964.

Goffman, Erving. Stigma. Englewood Cliffs, N.J.: Prentice Hall, 1963.

Goldfeld, Abraham. Diary of a Housing Manager. Chicago: National Association of Housing Officials, 1938.

Gordon, Milton M. Social Class in American Sociology. New York: McGraw Hill Book Co., 1958.

Hillery, George Jr. Communal Organizations: A Study of Total Societies. Chicago: University of Chicago Press, 1960.

Hipshman, Mae B. Public Housing at the Crossroads: The Boston Housing Authority. Boston Citizens Housing and Planning Association of Metropolitan Boston, 1967.

Ireland, Lola. Low-Income Life Styles. Washington, D.C.: U.S. Government Printing Office, 1968.

Isler, Morton L. Housing Management: A Progress Report. Washington, D.C.: The Urban Institute, 1970.

Kriesberg, Louis. Mothers In Poverty: A Study of Fatherless Families. Chicago: Aldine Publishing Co., 1970.

Lagey, Joseph,and Beverly Ayres. Community Treatment Programs for Multi-Problem Families. Vancouver, B.C.: Community Chest and Councils of Greater Vancouver Area, 1962.

Lemert, Edwin. Human Deviance, Social Problems and Social Control. Englewood Cliffs, N.J.: Prentice-Hall, 1967.

Lempert, Richard, and Kiyoshi Ikeda. "Evictions from Public Housing: Effects of Independent Review." American Sociological Review, October 1970.

Lewis, Harold, and Mildred Gwinessy. Helping the Poor Housekeeper in Public Housing. Philadelphia: Friends Neighborhood Guild, 1964.

Lewis, Oscar. "The Culture of Poverty." On Understanding Poverty. Edited by Daniel P. Moynihan. New York: Basic Books, 1968.

Meyerson, Martin, Barbara Terrett, and William L. Wheaton. Housing, People, and Cities. New York: McGraw-Hill Book Co., 1962.

_____, and Edward L. Banfield. Politics, Planning and the Public Interest: The Case of Public Housing in Chicago. New York: The Free Press, 1955.

Miller, Walter. "The Elimination of the American Lower Class as National Policy." On Understanding Poverty. Edited by Daniel P. Moynihan. New York: Basic Books, 1968.

Ministry of Cultural Affairs, Recreation and Social Welfare Department, The Netherlands. "Overijssel Family-Re-Adaptation Center." "Social Work Related to Problem Families and Neighborhoods in the Netherlands." 1966.

Ministry of Housing and Local Government. Unsatisfactory Tenants. London: Her Majesty's Stationery Office, 1955.

Moore, William, Jr. The Vertical Ghetto: Everyday Life in an Urban Project. New York: Random House, 1969.

National Association of Housing Officials. Housing Officials' Yearbook, 1936. Chicago, 1936.

National Association of Housing and Redevelopment Officials. Change for the Better. Washington, D.C., 1962.

National Urban League. The National Survey of Housing Abandonment. New York, 1972.

Newman, Oscar. "Physical Parameters of Defensible Space: Past Experience and Hypotheses." Mimeographed. New York: Columbia University, November 1959.

Parsons, Talcott, and Robert F. Balos. Family Socialization and Interaction Process. Glencoe, Illinois: The Free Press, 1955.

Pavenstedt, Eleanor. The Drifters: Children of Disorganized Lower-Class Families. Boston: Little Brown and Co., 1967.

Philip, A. F., and Noel Timms. The Problems of the Problem Family: A Critical Review of the Literature Concerning the Problem Family and Its Treatment. London: The Family Service Units, 1957.

Plager, Sheldon. "Policy Planning and the Courts; Judicial Review 1970." Journal of American Institute of Planners, May 1971.

"Problem Families." Journal of Housing, November 1959.

Rainwater, Lee. Behind Ghetto Walls: Black Family Life in a Federal Slum. Chicago: Aldine Publishing Co., 1970.

_____. "Fear and the House as Haven in the Lower Class." Journal of the American Institute of Planners 32 (1966).

_____. "Neutralizing the Disinherited: Some Psychological Aspects of Understanding the Poor." Occasional Paper number 30. Mimeographed. Washington University, 1967.

Rosahn, Beatrice, and Abraham Goldfeld. Housing Management Principles and Practices. Chicago: Covici Friede, 1937.

Rosow, Irving. Social Integration of the Aged. New York: The Free Press, 1967.

_____. "The Social Effects of the Physical Environment." Journal of the American Institute of Planners, May 1961.

Scheff, Thomas J. Being Mentally Ill: A Sociological Theory. Chicago: Aldine Publishing Co., 1966.

Schlesinger, Benjamin. The Multi-Problem Family: A Review and Annotated Bibliography. Toronto: University of Toronto Press, 1963.

Schorr, Alvin L. Slums and Social Insecurity. Washington, D.C.: U.S. Government Printing Office, 1963.

Scobie, Richard. "Residential Design for Tomorrow's Families— The Social Effects of Spatial Arrangements in Housing." Mimeographed. Waltham, Massachusetts: Florence Heller School for Advanced Studies in Social Welfare, 1970.

Seiler, Bernard R. "Problem Families Must Meet Standards Before Admission." Journal of Housing, February 1956.

Seltiz, Claire, Maril Jahoda, Morton Deutsch, and Stewart Cook. Research Methods in Social Relations. New York: Holt, Rinehart and Winston, 1964.

Shermer, George. More than Shelter: Social Needs in Low and Moderate Income Housing. Research Report No. 8 prepared for the Commission on Urban Problems. Washington D.C.: U.S. Government Printing Office, 1968.

_____. Public Housing is the Tenants: Rethinking Management's Role in Tenant and Community Relations. Washington D.C.: National Association of Housing and Redevelopment Officials, 1967.

Silverman, Abner. "Problem Families—Efforts at Social Rehabilitation Yield Results in Britain." Journal of Housing, February 1961.

_____. Administration of Publicly Owned Housing: Great Britain, Netherlands, and Sweden. U.S. Housing and Home Finance Agency. Washington, D.C.: U.S. Government Printing Office, 1961.

Starr, Roger. "Which of the Poor Shall Live in Public Housing." The Public Interest, Spring 1971.

Tannenbaum, Arnold S., and Jerald G. Bachman. "Structural Versus Individual Effects." American Journal of Sociology, May 1964.

Taube, Gerald. "The Social-Structural Sources of Residential Satisfaction-Dissatisfaction in Public Housing." Ph.D. Dissertation, Brandeis University, Waltham, Massachusetts, 1972.

Timms, Noel, and A. F. Philip. The Problem of the Problem Family: A Critical Review of the Literature Concerning the Problem Family and Its Treatment. London: Family Service Units, 1957.

U.S. Department of Health Education and Welfare and Housing and Home Finance Agency, Joint Task Force on Health, Education and Welfare Services and Housing. Two Year Progress Report. Washington, D.C.: U.S. Government Printing Office, 1965.

U.S. Department of Health, Education and Welfare. Services for Families Living in Public Housing. Washington D.C.: U.S. Government Printing Office, 1963.

U.S. Department of Housing and Urban Development. Renewal and
Housing Management Transmittal Notice RHM 7465.9 (2/22/71)
re: Grievance Procedures. Washington D.C.: U.S. Government Printing Office, 1971.

Valentine, Charles A. Culture and Poverty: Critique and Counter
Proposals. Chicago: University of Chicago Press, 1968.

Warren, Roland. Multi-Problem Families: A New Name or a New
Problem. New York: New York State Charities Aid Association, 1960.

_____. "A Multi-Problem Confrontation." The Multi-Problem
Dilemma. Edited by Gordon Brown. Metuchen, New Jersey:
Scarecrow Press, 1968.

Weinandy, Janet E., Lee J. Cary, M. O. Wagenfeld, and Charles V.
Willie. Working with the Poor. Syracuse N.Y.: Youth Development Center, 1965.

_____. Families Under Stress. Syracuse, N.Y.: Syracuse Youth
Development Center, 1962.

Whyte, William H., Jr., The Organization Man. Garden City, N.J.:
Doubleday, 1957.

Willie, Charles, and Janet Weinandy. "The Structure and Composition
of 'Problem' and 'Stable' Families in a Low-Income Population."
Marriage and Family Living, November 1963.

Wilson, James Q. "The Urban Unease." The Public Interest. Summer 1968.

Wood, Elizabeth, Housing Design: A Social Theory. New York:
Citizens Housing and Planning Council of New York, 1961.

Zuidplein Project. Rotterdam, The Netherlands: Municipal Welfare
Department of Rotterdam, 1953.

RELEVANT LEGAL DECISIONS

Chicago Housing Authority v. Steward. 237 N.E. 2d, 463, May 29, 1968.

Colon v. Thomkins Square Neighbors, Inc. 294 F Supp. 134 (S.D., New York, 1968).

Cleveland Metropolitan Housing Authority v. Patterson Ohio Court of Appeals. Cuyahoga County, July 10, 1963.

Holmes v. New York City Housing Authority. 398 F. 2d 262, July 18, 1968.

Lancaster Housing Authority v. Gardner. 211 Pa. Super. 502, 240, A. 2d 566. March 8, 1968.

Maringo v. New York City Housing Authority, No. 2197/1966 Superior Court of New York, August 8, 1966. (273, N.Y. S. 2d 1003).

Omaha Housing Authority v. U.S. Housing Authority (HUD), 468 F. 2d, 8th Cir., 1972.

Thomas et al. v. Housing Authority of the City of Little Rock, 35 U.S. L., W. 2722. E.D. Ark., 1967.

Thorpe v. Housing Authority of Durham, 383 U.S. 268 (1969).

Vinson v. Greenburgh Housing Authority. 288, N.Y. S. 2d 159. March 11, 1968.

ABOUT THE AUTHOR

RICHARD S. SCOBIE has worked with the social problems associated with low-income housing in both Latin America and the United States, as Community Development Consultant to the Housing Commission of Buenos Aires, Argentina; and, in Boston, as Director of Tenant and Community Relations for the Boston Housing Authority; staff director of the United Community Services Task Force on Services to Public Housing Neighborhoods; Chairperson of the Public Housing Committee of the Citizens Housing and Planning Association; and member of the Advisory Committee of the Massachusetts Housing Finance Agency.

Dr. Scobie holds a Ph.D. from Brandeis University, where this research was conducted, an M.S.W. from the University of Pittsburgh, and an A.B. from Dartmouth College. He has contributed to the Journal of Housing, The Public Interest, and a forthcoming book, Social Work in Public Service.

He is currently Executive Director of the Unitarian Universalist Service Committee, an international agency with headquarters in Boston, and President of the Massachusetts chapter of the National Association of Social Workers.

MANAGING LOW AND MODERATE INCOME
HOUSING
Edwin D. Abrams
and Edward B. Blackman

HOUSING THE POOR
edited by Donald J. Reeb
and James T. Kirk, Jr.

SOCIAL COSTS OF HUMAN UNDERDEVELOPMENT:
Case Study of Seven New York City Neighborhoods
Marvin Berkowitz

THE ECONOMICS OF RESIDENTIAL REHABILITA-
TION: Social Life of Housing in Harlem
Hyung C. Chung

RACIAL TRANSITION IN THE INNER SUBURBS:
Economic and Sociological Studies of the St. Louis
Area
edited by Solomon Sutker
and Sara Smith Sutker

PLANNING FOR THE LOWER EAST SIDE
Harry Schwartz,
assisted by Peter Abeles

NEW TOWNS AND COMMUNAL VALUES: A Case
Study of Columbia, Maryland
Richard Oliver Brooks

ARE NEW TOWNS FOR LOWER INCOME
AMERICANS TOO?
edited by John C. DeBoer
and Alexander Greendale